An Analysis of

Antonio Gramsci's

Prison Notebooks

Lorenzo Fusaro,
Jason Xidias
and
Adam Fabry

Published by Macat International Ltd
24:13 Coda Centre, 189 Munster Road, London SW6 6AW.

Distributed exclusively by Routledge
2 Park Square, Milton Park, Abingdon, Oxon OX14 4RN
711 Third Avenue, New York, NY 10017, USA

Routledge is an imprint of the Taylor & Francis Group, an informa business

www.macat.com
info@macat.com

Cataloguing in Publication Data
A catalogue record for this book is available from the British Library.
Library of Congress Cataloguing-in-Publication Data is available upon request.
Cover illustration: Etienne Gilfillan

ISBN 978-1-912303-26-7 (hardback)
ISBN 978-1-912127-42-9 (paperback)
ISBN 978-1-912282-14-2 (e-book)

Notice
The information in this book is designed to orientate readers of the work under analysis,
to elucidate and contextualise its key ideas and themes, and to aid in the development
of critical thinking skills. It is not meant to be used, nor should it be used, as a
substitute for original thinking or in place of original writing or research. References and
notes are provided for informational purposes and their presence does not constitute
endorsement of the information or opinions therein. This book is presented solely for
educational purposes. It is sold on the understanding that the publisher is not engaged
to provide any scholarly advice. The publisher has made every effort to ensure that
this book is accurate and up-to-date, but makes no warranties or representations with
regard to the completeness or reliability of the information it contains. The information
and the opinions provided herein are not guaranteed or warranted to produce particular
results and may not be suitable for students of every ability. The publisher shall not be
liable for any loss, damage or disruption arising from any errors or omissions, or from
the use of this book, including, but not limited to, special, incidental, consequential or
other damages caused, or alleged to have been caused, directly or indirectly, by the
information contained within.

CONTENTS

THE MACAT LIBRARY

The Macat Library is a series of unique academic explorations of seminal works in the humanities and social sciences – books and papers that have had a significant and widely recognised impact on their disciplines. It has been created to serve as much more than just a summary of what lies between the covers of a great book. It illuminates and explores the influences on, ideas of, and impact of that book. Our goal is to offer a learning resource that encourages critical thinking and fosters a better, deeper understanding of important ideas.

Each publication is divided into three Sections: Influences, Ideas, and Impact. Each Section has four Modules. These explore every important facet of the work, and the responses to it.

This Section-Module structure makes a Macat Library book easy to use, but it has another important feature. Because each Macat book is written to the same format, it is possible (and encouraged!) to cross-reference multiple Macat books along the same lines of inquiry or research. This allows the reader to open up interesting interdisciplinary pathways.

To further aid your reading, lists of glossary terms and people mentioned are included at the end of this book (these are indicated by an asterisk [*] throughout) – as well as a list of works cited.

Macat has worked with the University of Cambridge to identify the elements of critical thinking and understand the ways in which six different skills combine to enable effective thinking.
Three allow us to fully understand a problem; three more give us the tools to solve it. Together, these six skills make up the **PACIER** model of critical thinking. They are:

ANALYSIS – understanding how an argument is built
EVALUATION – exploring the strengths and weaknesses of an argument
INTERPRETATION – understanding issues of meaning

CREATIVE THINKING – coming up with new ideas and fresh connections
PROBLEM-SOLVING – producing strong solutions
REASONING – creating strong arguments

To find out more, visit **WWW.MACAT.COM.**

CRITICAL THINKING AND *PRISON NOTEBOOKS*

Primary critical thinking skill: ANALYSIS
Secondary critical thinking skill: REASONING

Antonio Gramsci's *Prison Notebooks* is a remarkable work, not only because it was written in jail as the Italian Marxist thinker fell victim to political oppression in his home country, but also because it shows his impressive analytical ability.

First published in 1948, 11 years after Gramsci's death, *Prison Notebooks* ably demonstrates that the writer has an innate ability to understand the relationship between different parts of an argument. This is how Gramsci manages to analyze such wide-ranging topics – capitalism, economics and culture – to explain historical developments. He introduces the idea of "hegemony," the means by which ruling classes in a society gain, keep hold of and manage their power, and, by carefully looking at how society operates, he reveals the manner in which the powerful deploy a combination of force and manipulation to convince most people that the existing social arrangement is logical and in their best interests – even when it isn't.

Gramsci shows exactly how the ruling class maintains power by influencing both political institutions like the courts and the police, and civil institutions, such as churches, family and schools. His powerful analysis led him to the conclusion that change can only take place in two ways, either through revolution or through a slow but constant struggle to transform the belief system of the ruling classes."

ABOUT THE AUTHOR OF THE ORIGINAL WORK

Antonio Gramsci was born in Sardinia, Italy, in 1891. While attending the University of Turin, he became interested in Marxist ideas. Soon he was participating in radical politics and writing for socialist newspapers, before co-founding the Italian Communist Party (PCI). After a visit to Russia, Gramsci returned to Italy to lead the political opposition to fascist dictator Benito Mussolini, which led to him being arrested and imprisoned. While in jail, he wrote and smuggled out the texts that would become Prison Notebooks, a collection of his ideas, theories, and arguments. The work would not be published until after Gramsci's death in 1937, but Prison Notebooks has since become hugely influential in a range of academic fields, including philosophy, sociology, and international relations.

ABOUT THE AUTHORS OF THE ANALYSIS

Lorenzo Fusaro did his postgraduate research at King's College London and is currently a member of the Department of Economics at the Universidad Autónoma Metropolitana-Azcapotzalco in Mexico.

Dr Jason Xidias holds a PhD in European Politics from King's College London, where he completed a comparative dissertation on immigration and citizenship in Britain and France. He was also a Visiting Fellow in European Politics at the University of California, Berkeley. Currently, he is Lecturer in Political Science at New York University.

Dr Adam Fabry is currently doing postdoctoral research at CIECS-CONICET-UNC in Argentina. He has studied at the Universidad Nacional de Quilmes, the UNLP-Universidad Nacional de La Plata, and Brunel University. His main research interest is the comparative political economy of neoliberalism in Eastern Europe and Latin America.

ABOUT MACAT

GREAT WORKS FOR CRITICAL THINKING

Macat is focused on making the ideas of the world's great thinkers accessible and comprehensible to everybody, everywhere, in ways that promote the development of enhanced critical thinking skills.

It works with leading academics from the world's top universities to produce new analyses that focus on the ideas and the impact of the most influential works ever written across a wide variety of academic disciplines. Each of the works that sit at the heart of its growing library is an enduring example of great thinking. But by setting them in context – and looking at the influences that shaped their authors, as well as the responses they provoked – Macat encourages readers to look at these classics and game-changers with fresh eyes. Readers learn to think, engage and challenge their ideas, rather than simply accepting them.

WAYS IN TO THE TEXT

KEY POINTS

- Today, Antonio Gramsci (1891–1937) is considered one of the most important Marxist* thinkers; Marxism, the political and economic theory of the nineteenth-century economist Karl Marx,* has offered an extremely influential analysis of the struggle between social classes and possible solutions for a more equal society.

- Gramsci's *Prison Notebooks*, first published in Italian in 1948, explains how the ruling class*—the group of people who can exert the most power and authority in a society—manipulate ideas to gain and keep power.

- Many of Gramsci's concepts still influence how social scientists today think about societies.

Who was Antonio Gramsci?

Antonio Gramsci, the author of *Prison Notebooks* (1948), was born on the Italian island of Sardinia in 1891. His politics were influenced by his older brother, Gennaro,* a socialist* activist; socialism is a political and economic system that calls for resources to be shared between all members of society. While living together at Dettori Lyceum (a secondary school) in Cagliari, Italy, the Gramsci brothers became interested in socialist politics, frequently participating in events organized by local factory workers.

In 1911, after finishing at Dettori Lyceum, Gramsci won a prestigious scholarship to attend the University of Turin. There, he took courses in linguistics (the structure and functioning of languages), the humanities (an exploration of culture in its many aspects), and social sciences (an area of study concerned with society), and he learned more about communist* ideas. Communism is a political and economic system in which workers own and operate the means of production*—that is, the resources and technology necessary for making goods and services. Eventually, in a communist system, social classes and the idea of the state itself will fade away.

Additionally, while at the University of Turin, Gramsci became friends with many prominent socialist and communist thinkers, such as Angelo Tasca,* who would become a founding member of the Italian Communist Party* (or PCI). Later in life, Tasca and Gramsci would disagree over fascism,* a system of government that involves a dictator having extreme power, and which emphasizes nationalism and military strength.

In 1915, while working as a militant journalist, Gramsci joined the Italian Socialist Party* (or PSI). Both his writing and his speeches at workers' meetings influenced people around the country.

In March 1917, the leader of Russia, Tsar* Nicolas II,* was overthrown in the first of two Russian Revolutions* that year. The second revolution, in October, led to a communist government and eventually to the Soviet Union* (a federation of countries in Eastern Europe and Asia that called themselves "communist," though some have disputed whether they actually were). Also referred to as the "Bolshevik"* revolution, after the political faction led by workers known as the Bolsheviks, it helped convinced Gramsci that similar transformations needed to happen in capitalist* countries. Capitalism, an economic system that emphasizes private ownership and management of resources, was for Gramsci a profoundly unfair, unethical way of arranging a society.

In 1921, Gramsci and fellow Italian Marxist Amadeo Bordiga* left the Italian Socialist Party to found the Italian Communist Party (PCI). The PCI would play a major role in resisting the influence of fascism. It was powerful enough that it was outlawed by Benito Mussolini,* who led Italy between 1922 and 1943.

In 1929, Mussolini's fascist police arrested and imprisoned Gramsci. He remained in jail until 1935, when he was released because of poor health. Two years later, he died in Rome. He did not live long enough to see *Prison Notebooks* published.

Today, Gramsci is widely regarded as one of the foremost Marxist theorists, and as one of the great thinkers of the social sciences. His work has influenced a range of academic disciplines, including political science, history, philosophy, and sociology* (the study of society and social behavior).

What Does *Prison Notebooks* Say?

In *Prison Notebooks*, Gramsci explains why socialism took hold in Russia after the revolution, but not in Italy and Western Europe. He also tries to provide guidance for workers.

Before Gramsci, the German political philosopher and economist Karl Marx had argued that the ruling classes used coercion* (the threat of force) and consent* (manipulating people into believing that the existing system is natural and beneficial) to get the most labor out of workers, which led to higher profits. Gramsci builds on this in *Prison Notebooks* by introducing the idea of hegemony.* Hegemony refers to how ruling classes in a society gain, keep, and manage their power.

More specifically, Gramsci explains that the ruling classes maintain their hegemony through coercion and consent. In various ways, he argues, they are able to make people believe that the way things are is the way things should be—even when the ways things are is not in their interest. For example, the ruling class might treat workers unfairly in order to profit from their labor, but through coercion and consent, they convince those workers that this is the natural order of things—or that the way things are is based on common sense.*

Gramsci's discussion of hegemony also depends upon another idea: the integral state.* The integral state is the idea that the ruling classes rely on a combination of social institutions to maintain their power and control. For example, some institutions are political, such as the court system and the police, and some are civil, such as churches, families, and schools. In using the term "integrated state," Gramsci emphasizes that the ruling class maintains power by influencing both political and civil institutions.[1]

It was important to Gramsci to do more than simply describe how the ruling classes maintain and exercise their power. He also wanted to lay out political strategies that could be used to change the system.

He therefore discusses two ways in which revolutionary change takes place: through a war of maneuver* or a war of position.* By "war of maneuver," Gramsci means revolution—a popular uprising resulting in the overthrow of the present system. By "war of position," he means a slow but constant struggle to transform the belief system of the ruling classes. Both of these, he argues, are strategies for transforming a society.

Gramsci believed that the correct strategy depended on where the revolution was happening: the war of maneuver was better for countries in Eastern Europe, and the war of position was more appropriate for Central and Western Europe. As Gramsci notes in one of the most-cited statements in *Prison Notebooks* (written in November–December 1930), "In the East, the State was everything, civil society was primordial and gelatinous; in the West, there was a proper relationship between State and civil society."[2]

Gramsci came up with these two strategies based on his interest in and experience of history. Particularly important for him were the various revolutions that swept through Europe in the early twentieth century. These included the Russian Revolution, the rise of fascism, and the factory council movements,* in which Italian workers defended their interests against the ruling classes.

Readers of *Prison Notebooks* should keep in mind that Gramsci wrote them against the backdrop of World War I,* a global war from 1914 to 1918 in which 16 million people were killed. Other important historical developments that informed his work were the Great Depression* (a period of economic instability, unemployment, and falling living standards that began in the United States in 1929), and "Fordism,"* an economic system based on mass production (industrialized manufacturing, conducted in great numbers) and consumption (purchasing and use) that developed in the United States.

Why Does *Prison Notebooks* Matter?

Gramsci wrote *Prison Notebooks* from prison after the fascist dictator Benito Mussolini ordered his arrest. He spent the period from 1929 to 1935 working on it before poor health forced him to stop, leaving it unfinished. Despite this inauspicious beginning, it was eventually published, translated, and read all over the world.[3]

Prison Notebooks, which includes 33 notebooks and more than 2,300 pages, covers a range of subjects including politics, history, philosophy, sociology, economics, and education. Gramsci's ideas helped shape the political strategies of the Italian Communist Party (PCI) during the 1970s. Since then, they have inspired generations of activists and scholars.

Gramsci's influence is not limited to Marxists though. As the British historian Eric Hobsbawm* has observed, he is also one of the great social scientists.[4] Readers today should see his work as important both politically and intellectually.

Nowadays, many of Gramsci's most important ideas are quite

relevant. These include coercion, consent, hegemony, and the crisis of hegemony,* or how the ruling class responds when people become dissatisfied with the social arrangement and threaten to revolt.

NOTES

1   Peter Thomas, *The Gramscian Moment: Philosophy, Hegemony and Marxism* (Leiden: Brill, 2009), 137.

2   Antonio Gramsci, *Selections from the Prison Notebooks*, ed. and trans. Quintin Hoare and John Mathews (London: Lawrence & Wishart, 1971), Q7, §16, 238.

3   Gramsci, *Selections from the Prison Notebooks*.

4   Eric Hobsbawm, *Gramsci in Europa e in America*, ed. Antonio Santonucci (Roma: Laterza, 1995).

SECTION 1
INFLUENCES

MODULE 1
THE AUTHOR AND THE
HISTORICAL CONTEXT

KEY POINTS

- *Prison Notebooks* is a foundational work of political and social theory.

- During Gramsci's university years in Turin, he encountered the writing of the Italian philosophers Benedetto Croce* and Giovanni Gentile* and became interested in radical politics.

- Gramsci wrote during a time in which Italy—and much of Europe—was undergoing political instability and social upheaval.

Why Read This Text?

The first edition of *Prison Notebooks* was published in Italian in 1948, 11 years after Antonio Gramsci's death. Since then, generations of Marxists* and other political activists have been fascinated by it. "Marxism" is the political and economic philosophy of the nineteenth-century political philosopher Karl Marx;* it calls for workers to own and operate the means of production* (the resources required for entities such as industry) and to overthrow the social and economic system of capitalism* dominant in the West today.

The text has attracted attention for the way it analyzes hegemony,* or the system by which the ruling classes in a society gain, keep, and wield power. It is also important for how it develops Marxist principles, its insights into culture, how citizens can unite to resist those in power, and for Gramsci's discussion of capitalism—an economic system in which resources and the

❝ I turn and turn in my cell like a fly that doesn't know where to die. ❞

Antonio Gramsci, *Selections from the Prison Notebooks*

production of goods and services are privately owned.

Gramsci's *Prison Notebooks* has had an impact in a range of fields, including history, political science, economics, philosophy, sociology,* and education. Many have analyzed and built on his ideas. In fact, there is a name for the various schools of thought that have developed from his work: "Gramscianism." As the Marxist philosopher and renowned Gramscian scholar Peter Thomas* points out, "This popularity and diffusion are all the more remarkable when the relative neglect into which other authors from the Marxist tradition have fallen in the same period is recalled."[1]

Though Gramsci died in 1937, his writing is still relevant. Today, the world is recovering from the Great Recession* (a severe economic downturn that began after the US housing market collapsed in 2007), millions of people are struggling to find work, and fierce political battles are being fought over how government should be organized. All of these are issues Gramsci addressed. It is therefore likely that his writing will continue to receive attention in the future.

Author's Life

Gramsci was born in 1891 in a small town in Sardinia, which was then (and is still) one of the poorest regions in Italy. His youth was marked by health problems and poverty.

He would eventually receive a prestigious scholarship that allowed him to attend the University of Turin in northern Italy. During this time, he encountered the writing of the philosophers Benedetto Croce and Giovanni Gentile. Their work encouraged him to become interested in radical politics.

In 1919, he joined fellow Italian Marxists Angelo Tasca,* Umberto Terracini,* and Palmiro Togliatti* in founding a socialist newspaper, *L'Ordine Nuovo.** Two years later, they also created the Italian Communist Party,* or PCI. Then, in 1922, Gramsci went to Moscow as a PCI representative at the Third International,* an international organization of Marxist groups. While there, he learned more about the core principles of Marxism, and also about leading Marxist theorists, such as Vladimir Lenin* (a leader in the Russian Revolution of 1917* and founder of the Russian Communist Party).

When Gramsci returned to Italy in 1924, he was tasked with turning the PCI into a political party that could oppose dictator Benito Mussolini.* Mussolini governed under a system called fascism,* which emphasized extreme loyalty to one's country, military strength, and the state's control over all aspects of society. In 1926, he had Gramsci arrested as part of a crackdown against those who opposed him.

Readers should recognize Gramsci's arrest as evidence of how successful he was politically. For example, during the trial, the fascist prosecutor remarked that Gramsci was a danger to the current government, declaring, "We must prevent this brain from working for twenty years."[2]

Author's Background

Gramsci's philosophy was certainly shaped by his childhood experiences with poverty and his education. However, the circumstances that led to his incarceration must have been painful for him: Mussolini was systematically stamping out those who resisted him. For example, it was on his orders that the revolutionary workers movement* was violently crushed.

The revolutionary workers movement had been important to Gramsci because of its role in a period known as the Biennio Rosso,* or "red biennium" (red is a color historically associated with socialism* and communism,* and "biennium" simply means two years). During this time, huge numbers of workers participated in strikes, occupied factories, and resisted Mussolini's fascist rule. These were, of course, political strategies and goals that Gramsci believed in.

Italy was not the only country experiencing severe social upheaval during this time. In the years after World War I,* which was fought between 1914 and 1918, many countries in Europe experienced economic crises, political instability, and even violent resistance to the established governments. In Russia, these forces ultimately led to the Russian Revolution, in which the Russian leader, Tsar* Nicolas II,* was overthrown, and the world's first socialist government was established.

NOTES

1 Peter Thomas, *The Gramscian Moment: Philosophy, Hegemony and Marxism* (Leiden: Brill, 2009), xvii.

2 Carlos Nelson Coutinho, *Gramsci's Political Thought* (Leiden: Brill, 2012), 47.

MODULE 2
ACADEMIC CONTEXT

KEY POINTS

- While studying at the University of Turin, Antonio Gramsci encountered the writing of philosophers Benedetto Croce* and Giovanni Gentile,* which helped him understand the important relationship between culture and politics.

- Later, Gramsci went to Moscow to participate in the Third International,* an international organization of Marxist* groups. Here, he encountered the ideas of other revolutionary thinkers.

- During the Russian Revolution* of 1917, Russian Marxists had used the term "hegemony"* to refer to how the ruling class* exercised power over the working classes (and society in general).

The Work in its Context

In *Prison Notebooks*, Gramsci builds on the ideas of the German philosopher and economist Karl Marx.* In order to better understand Gramsci's work, it is, then, helpful to understand Marx's.

Marx claimed that societies were made up of two parts: the base* and the superstructure.* By base, Marx meant the various economic relationships that make up daily life, such as working conditions and property ownership. By superstructure, he meant both a society's beliefs and culture, and its various institutions—police and education systems, for example.

According to Marx, the base economic relationships shape the superstructure. And importantly, the superstructure—a society's

❝ [Karl Marx's Preface to the *Critique of Political Economy*] is the most important authentic source for the reconstruction of the Philosophy of Praxis.**❞**

Antonio Gramsci, *Selections from the Prison Notebooks*

values, culture, its type of government—tend to reflect the interests of the ruling classes.

Based on these ideas, Marx argued that if workers became aware that a society's base and superstructure did not reflect their interests, they might join together to transform their society into something new. To do this, they would try to overthrow the base (the "normal" way that everyday economic relationships happened). This would lead to the replacement of capitalism,* a system in which resources and services are privately owned, with communism,* a system whereby workers control the means of production* and the state and social classes would cease to exist.

After Marx's death in 1883, working-class movements across Europe joined together to form the Second International* (which was, like the Third International that followed it, an international organization of Marxist groups). The Second International defended Marx's ideas, for instance, that the base determined a society's superstructure. They also believed that because of this relationship, the economic problems that accompanied capitalism would ultimately lead to its being replaced.

However, the members of the Second International had difficulty unifying. Their troubles were made worse when World War I began, as nationalism* (extraordinary devotion to one's country) caused divisions, and the organization dissolved in 1916.

This did not, however, mean that Marxism itself stopped evolving. Indeed, Vladimir Lenin,* the leader of the Russian Revolution, founded the Third International in 1919. It was to this organization's vision of Marxism that Gramsci's *Prison Notebooks* responded.

Overview of the Field

The Second International's failure offered an important lesson. The group had not been able to understand why there had been a revolution in Russia, but not elsewhere in Europe. A new way of understanding Marxist principles was therefore needed. In addition, Gramsci was writing during a time marked by economic and political crises, and he wanted to address these challenges.

Other revolutionary socialists during this time argued that the Second International had misinterpreted and oversimplified Marxist principles. These included such important voices as Vladimir Lenin, the leader of the Bolsheviks in the Russian Revolution and founder of the Russian Communist Party; Leon Trotsky,* a revolutionary who wrote several important Marxist works; and Rosa Luxemburg,* a Marxist thinker and author of, among other works, *Accumulation of Capital* (1951).

Gramsci associated himself with these figures. Readers can see this connection most clearly in his article "The Revolution Against Capital," which was written on the eve of the Russian Revolution. In it, Gramsci argues that the Russian Revolution had been driven by different principles from those emphasized by Marxists of the Second International.

Academic Influences

One of Gramsci's earliest influences was his older brother Gennaro,* who introduced him to socialist* ideas. Gennaro was a militant member of the Italian Socialist Party* (PSI), and often sent Gramsci copies of *Avanti!,* the party's official newspaper.

Another important influence was the wave of social unrest that swept Sardinia (an island off Italy's western coast) in the early 1900s.

Gramsci watched as protesters were brutally repressed by Italian troops. According to the editors and translators of *Prison Notebooks*, Quintin Hoare and Geoffrey N. Smith, "The form taken by the repression, both military and legal, gave a great impetus to the cause of Sardinian nationalism, and it was to this cause that Gramsci first adhered."[1]

At the University of Turin, Gramsci read the work of the Italian philosophers Benedetto Croce and Giovanni Gentile. These writers helped him think about the importance of culture and ideas to political and economic systems. Gramsci also encountered the output of the Italian Marxist Antonio Labriola,* whose ideas influenced many in the early twentieth century.

In addition to his studies, Gramsci began to take a more active role in politics. He worked as a journalist for several socialist newspapers, including *Il Grido del Popolo** and *Avanti!* Eventually, he and fellow Marxists Angelo Tasca,* Umberto Terracini,* and Palmiro Togliatti* would found their own socialist newspaper, *L'Ordine Nuovo.** In its pages, they advocated for workers to come together and form workers' councils,* just as they had in Russia, so that they could negotiate for better working conditions.

In 1921, the same group that had founded *L'Ordine Nuovo* helped found the Italian Communist Party* (PCI), and Gramsci was elected one of the party's officials. The following year, he went to Moscow to represent the PCI in the Third International. While there, he learned more about important Marxist ideas, especially those of Vladimir Lenin. In fact, some of these ideas would become central concepts in *Prison Notebooks.*

NOTES

1   Antonio Gramsci, *Selections from the Prison Notebooks*, ed. and trans. Quintin Hoare and Geoffrey N. Smith (London: Lawrence & Wishart, 1971), xix. See also Carlos Nelson Coutinho, *Gramsci's Political Thought* (Leiden: Brill, 2012), 2.

MODULE 3
THE PROBLEM

KEY POINTS

- During Gramsci's time, Marxists* sought to answer the question of why a revolution like the one that occurred in Russia in 1917 had not occurred elsewhere in Europe.

- Gramsci wrote about culture and ideology from a historical materialist* position—that is, he focused heavily on how economics affected the way society was set up; in taking this perspective, he drew on the ideas of Karl Marx,* the Russian revolutionary and thinker Vladimir Lenin,* and other contemporary Marxists.

- The concept of hegemony,* or how the ruling class* maintains power over others in society, was central to Gramsci's political theory.

Core Question

Antonio Gramsci's *Prison Notebooks* should be considered in the light of the author's two main concerns. First, Gramsci wanted to know why there had been a revolution in Russia, but not in other parts of Europe. Second, he wanted to develop a theory and strategies that would help the working class overthrow the social and economic system of capitalism,* along with the system of politics and values that propped it up. For Gramsci (and Marxists in general), the economic arrangement in capitalism, in which a few people control resources, land, and technology—"the means of production"*—is profoundly unfair for the vast majority of society.

The Russian Revolution began in 1917 when Vladimir Lenin led the Bolsheviks*—a Russian political faction composed of revolutionary

❝ It may be ruled out that immediate economic crises of themselves produce fundamental historical events; they can simply create a terrain more favorable to the dissemination of certain modes of thought, and certain ways of posing and resolving questions involving the entire subsequent development of national life. **❞**

Antonio Gramsci, *Selections from the Prison Notebooks*

workers, in the main—in an uprising to overthrow Tsar* Nicolas II.* Ultimately, the Bolsheviks were victorious, and established a socialist* government, in which resources were held in common hands.

However, in other European countries, radical leftist groups (that is, groups with politics similar to the Bolsheviks') were not able to stage successful revolutions. This encouraged Gramsci to try to answer the question of what had been different in Russia. As the Brazilian professor of political theory Carlos Coutinho* puts it, Gramsci tried to respond to the question of "why, in spite of the serious economic crisis and of the apparently revolutionary situation in a large part of Western Europe in [this] period ... was it not possible to successfully repeat the victorious experience of the Bolsheviks in Russia?"[1]

However, as the Gramsci scholar Peter Thomas* points out, this was not the only important aspect of Gramsci's work. He also wanted to develop Marxist ideas and to give workers strategies to challenge capitalism and the system of politics and beliefs that sustained it.

Prison Notebooks, Thomas continues, represents an "attempt to elaborate a political theory which would ... shape and guide ... the popular ... classes' attempts to awaken from the nightmares of their histories and to assume social and political leadership."[2] In other words, *Prison Notebooks* was an attempt to help Marxists overcome setbacks they had suffered following World War I.*

The Participants

Previously, Marxist thinkers had emphasized that power in a society came from controlling economic relationships. Gramsci extended this approach, often called "historical materialism," to encompass culture and ideas too. Gramsci firmly believed that culture and economics could not be separated—a belief influenced by the writing of Italian philosopher Benedetto Croce.*

Croce's historiographies* (or writing about history) had impressed Gramsci. He felt that Croce had "energetically drawn attention to the importance of facts concerning culture and thought in the development of history."[3] Additionally, he was influenced by how Croce wrote about intellectuals, relationships in civil society* (private institutions such as churches and families), and especially hegemony.

Croce's writing also encouraged Gramsci to see how important private lives were to a society. For example, though courts of law might seem to best represent the power of the ruling classes, Croce argued that in reality, their power also regulated citizens' private lives—family and religious relationships, for example.

Readers should note that Karl Marx, the father of Marxism, had also written about both economics and culture. Marx argued, for example, that economic conflicts matter only if people recognize them as problems. In other words, if an economic arrangement is seen as normal within a society, nobody will object to it—even if it is unfair.[4]

Gramsci, however, would go much further in writing about the relationship between culture and economics.

The Contemporary Debate

One of Gramsci's most important concepts was hegemony, or how the ruling class gained, kept, and used power. Lenin had used this term during the Russian Revolution to describe what the working classes were fighting against and how they should seek to gain power, and Gramsci further investigated and explained it.

One way in particular in which Gramsci analyzed hegemony was to begin with Marx's idea that economics and culture were linked, and to examine culture's role in this pairing more closely than Marx had. For Gramsci, ideology (that is, political assumptions or philosophy), culture, and politics are of the utmost importance. Economic problems do not automatically provoke people to challenge the social order in which they live: they lead only to the potential for a revolution. Therefore, important cultural shifts must also occur.

Based on this, Gramsci argued that communist* thinkers could demonstrate to the working classes how the bourgeoisie* (a Marxist term for the ruling class) exercised hegemony over them. Gramsci believed that educating working-class people—and encouraging them to actively resist—might lead to what he called a crisis of hegemony,* in which the ruling classes were not able to maintain their authority. He also hoped that education could inspire alliances between, for example, industrial and agricultural workers. Such alliances were necessary, he believed, if capitalism was to be overthrown.

Finally, readers should note that Gramsci was writing during a turbulent time in history. World War I had ravaged huge parts of Europe and fueled new political movements, such as fascism* and socialism. The United States was emerging as the leading world power. And the Great Depression,* an economic crisis that began in the United States in 1929, created unemployment and poor standards of living across the world. It was important to communist thinkers during this time to try to understand these events.

For example, Gramsci wrote about Americanism,* the version of capitalism that developed in the US, and Fordism,* the mass production of goods and services. American capitalism, he claimed, would be most successful in the long run. This is why he argued that the Great Depression, as bad as it was for so many people, would not cause the crisis of hegemony that would end capitalism.

NOTES

1   Carlos Nelson Coutinho, *Gramsci's Political Thought* (Leiden: Brill, 2012), 50.

2   Peter Thomas, *The Gramscian Moment: Philosophy, Hegemony and Marxism* (Leiden: Brill, 2009), 159.

3   Antonio Gramsci, *Quaderni del carcere*, ed. Felice Platone (Torino: Einaudi, 1948–51), Q. 10, 1211.

4   Gramsci, *Quaderni*, Q. 13, 2592.

MODULE 4
THE AUTHOR'S CONTRIBUTION

KEY POINTS

- Gramsci built his argument on the traditional Marxist* idea that unfair economic relationships (economic ties between individuals and social classes) and culture were linked.

- Gramsci's most important contribution is his concept of hegemony*—how the ruling classes* convince the working classes that society is arranged as it should be, even when that arrangement is unfair for most people.

- *Prison Notebooks* provides important tools for understanding how capitalist* societies work, and offers the means by which those who want to transform society can do so.

Author's Aims

While Antonio Gramsci, the author of *Prison Notebooks*, was arrested in early November 1926 because of his political opposition to the Italian fascist* dictator Benito Mussolini,* he did not stop working because he was in jail. Instead, he decided to focus on "intensively and systematically" developing the ideas of Marxism. It could, he believed, help him understand why revolutions, such as the one in Russia, had not worked in Europe.[1]

This was a question that interested communist* organizations all over the world, including the Third International,* an international organization of Marxist groups. Therefore, while Gramsci was not able to actively participate in workers' movements, he was still able to help Marxist groups better understand how capitalist societies worked and how they could be challenged.

Today, we remember Gramsci for these contributions. However,

❝ A social group can, indeed must, already exercise 'leadership' before winning governmental power (this is indeed one of the principal conditions for the winning of such power); it subsequently becomes dominant when it exercises power, but even if it holds it firmly in its grasp, it must continue to 'lead' as well. ❞

Antonio Gramsci, *Selections from the Prison Notebooks*

it is also worth noting that *Prison Notebooks* was personal as well as political. In a letter to his sister-in-law Tatiana Schucht,* Gramsci said that he wrote *Prison Notebooks* because he wanted to "give a focus to [his] inner life," and to articulate his beliefs in a form that would last.

Approach

Those who have studied the 33 *Prison Notebooks* have shown that Gramsci had a clear plan for the work as a whole.[2] For example, in the first *Notebook*, Gramsci lists 16 points that he will develop as he writes. Although a health crisis in 1931 convinced him to stray from this plan, it remained important in his future reflections.[3]

In the eighth notebook of 1932, Gramsci lays out a table of contents for what he called his "special notebooks." From this, we can see that he intended to explore philosophy (*Notebook 11*), and relatedly, to comment on the writings of Benedetto Croce* (*Notebook 10*). These would prepare him to write about politics and hegemony (*Notebook 13*).

He also explored the history of groups that had been oppressed (*Notebook 25*), Italian history (*Notebook 19*), and the specific form of capitalism developing in the United States (*Notebook 22*).[4]

Contribution in Context

Readers should remember that Gramsci was not exploring all of these ideas simply for their own sake. He wanted to find a way to improve upon the Marxist ideas of the Second International,* which had failed, with the organization dissolving in 1916. In particular, he wanted to focus on how economic relationships are related to culture.

To do this, Gramsci drew on an important concept from Karl Marx's* "Preface to A Contribution to the Critique of Political Economy" (1859).[5] Marx wrote that everyday economic relationships, or the base,* shape and influence a society's political beliefs and values, which he called the superstructure.* According to Marx, this was how capitalist societies worked: the ruling class controlled the base, and were therefore able to convince people that society was working as it should be, even if it was unfair for many.

Gramsci also learned from Vladimir Lenin.* Lenin's experience of leading the Russian Revolution* in 1917 taught him that it was important for Marxist leaders to understand the relationship between the base and the superstructure in order for the revolution to work.

Finally, Gramsci drew on Croce's writing about history. Croce showed how history could be analyzed through culture, and this encouraged Gramsci to see culture as particularly influential.

All of these sources led Gramsci to argue that a society's superstructure—its values and beliefs—could influence its base. In doing so, he broke away from the traditional argument that the base determined the superstructure. He claimed instead that each could influence the other.

As a consequence, while economic developments (such as economic downturns and depressions) could lead to a revolution, cultural and political developments might also do so. Additionally, a revolution's success might depend on changes to both the economic relationships and cultural beliefs.

All of this returns us to the concept of hegemony. Hegemony, for Gramsci, means that a ruling class controls both economic relationships and cultural values.

Hegemony is an idea that he continued to develop over the course of the *Notebooks*,[6] and it is interesting to think about the consequences of Gramsci's time in prison on his work. For example, hegemony does not appear at all in his writing before being jailed. While he did write about the importance of understanding "superstructures" in a letter to the Communist Party of the Soviet Union* (a federation of countries in Eastern Europe and Asia that called themselves "communist"), this was a long way from the understanding of hegemony that he eventually reached in *Prison Notebooks*.[7]

NOTES

1 Carlos Nelson Coutinho, *Gramsci's Political Thought* (Leiden: Brill, 2012), 50.

2 Raul Mordenti, "Quaderni del carcere di Antonio Gramsci," in *Letteratura Italina Einaudi, le opera*, Vol. IV/II, ed. Alberto Asor Rosa (Torino: Einaudi, 1996).

3 Alberto Burgio, *Per Gramsci: Crisi e potenza del moderno* (Roma: Derive Approdi, 2007), 50–1.

4 Mordenti, "Quaderni del carcere di Antonio Gramsci."

5 Karl Marx, "Preface to a Contribution to the Critique of Political Economy," in *Marx/Engels Collected Works* (*MECW*), Vol. 29 (London: Lawrence & Wishart, and New York: International Publishers, 1975–2005). Other important texts on which Gramsci would rely are Marx's historical analysis of France in "The Eighteenth Brumaire of Louis Bonaparte," *MECW*, Vol. 11, and of course the three volumes of Marx, *Capital*, *MECW*, Vols 35–7.

6 Giuseppe Cospito, "Egemonia," in *Le parole di Gramsci*, ed. Fabio Frosini and Guido Liguori (Roma: Carocci, 2004).

7 Coutinho, *Gramsci's Political Thought*, 38–41.

SECTION 2
IDEAS

MODULE 5
MAIN IDEAS

KEY POINTS

- Important themes in *Prison Notebooks* are hegemony;* the crisis of hegemony,* which refers to the working classes questioning the legitimacy of the ruling class;* and the integral state,* or the idea that the ruling classes control both public and private institutions in order to keep the existing social order intact.

- When a crisis of hegemony occurs, the ruling classes will try to reform the capitalist system so that the majority of people will keep faith in the social order.

- Gramsci's main argument is that the ruling classes attain and maintain hegemony by using coercion* (the threat of force) and consent* (manipulating people into believing that the existing system is natural and beneficial).

Key Themes

Antonio Gramsci died in 1937, leaving *Prison Notebooks* unfinished. Scholars today must therefore be careful when they make claims about what Gramsci believed. It is possible, after all, that he would have continued to develop or revise his ideas.

One idea that can guide Gramscians (scholars or followers of Gramsci) is his "philosophy of praxis,"* which he describes in *Notebooks 10* and *11*.[1] Philosophy of praxis is the idea that both economics *and* culture are important for understanding how the ruling class rule. In coming to this conclusion, Gramsci built upon the thinking of both Karl Marx* and one of Marx's greatest influences, the German philosopher Georg Wilhelm Friedrich

❝ [T]he philosophy of praxis is a reform and a development of Hegelianism; it is a philosophy that has been liberated (or is attempting to liberate itself) from any unilateral and fanatical ideological elements; it is consciousness full of contradictions, in which the philosopher himself, understood both individually and as an entire social group, not only grasps the contradictions, but posits himself as an element of the contradiction and elevates this element to a principal of knowledge and therefore of action. 'Man in general,' in whatever form he presents himself, is denied and all dogmatically 'unitary' concepts are spurned and destroyed as expressions of the concept of 'man in general' or of 'human nature' imminent in every man. ❞

Antonio Gramsci, *Selections from the Prison Notebooks*

Hegel* (1770–1831), who had written about culture.

The "philosophy of praxis" helps scholars understand what Gramsci means by hegemony—the idea that the ruling classes maintain and exercise power by manipulating people into believing that the current political and economic arrangement is in their best interest, when in reality it is only in the best interest of the minority.

Gramsci links hegemony with the idea of the integral state. The integral state refers to the combination of political organizations (such as the courts of law) and civil organizations (such as churches and schools) through which the ruling classes exert their control.

Another term linked with hegemony is the "crisis of hegemony," or the idea that as the working classes become aware that they are being taken advantage of, the ruling classes will suffer a crisis of hegemony, in which the working classes resist being controlled and manipulated.

Finally, Gramsci's writing about hegemony also forms the foundation of his advice to political revolutionaries. He offers advice for Marxists* who want to resist and overcome systems of government.

Exploring the Ideas

Readers should remember that Gramsci did not invent the term "hegemony." In fact, it had been used by the Greek philosopher Aristotle* 2,000 or so years before to refer to a "supreme leader."[2] Vladimir Lenin* also used it when he argued that people in a society who suffered because of the way the ruling classes maintained their hegemony should come together to revolt.[3]

Gramsci's most important innovation was his detailed description of exactly how people in power maintained their hegemony over others. For Gramsci, hegemony was exercised through both economic relationships and cultural beliefs. If most people believed that society was arranged in the best way that it possibly could be—even if this was not actually true—then they would also accept factors such as unfair wages and working conditions.

The idea that society is kept stable because people believe it's the best possible option is a particularly important part of Gramsci's argument. He argued that coercion—the threat of force through control of groups such as the police and the army—was not enough to maintain control. True power also came from persuading most people to accept that how society was arranged was more or less the best possible arrangement.

Gramsci used these conclusions to come up with strategies for how the people in power could be overthrown and society transformed. He offered two possible routes to revolution: a war of maneuver,* in which people attacked the organizations that helped those in power stay in power, and a war of position,* whereby revolutionaries worked slowly and steadily to shift cultural beliefs in their favor.

Gramsci argues that a war of position would be more effective. While a war of maneuver offers the chance to quickly overthrow a government, it would not necessarily change cultural beliefs on the best way to set up a society. As Gramsci put it, the "powerful system of fortresses and earthworks" would still be owned and controlled by the bourgeoisie* (a Marxist term for the ruling class). That is, if people believe that the existing society is the best possible option, then a revolution might result in a society with new leaders, but which looks and operates exactly as the old one did.

In light of this, Gramsci argued that a successful revolution also involves a cultural revolution: society must adopt new morals and values so that when the existing order is overthrown, it will be prepared to set up a new social order. In Gramsci's eyes, that new social order was communism.*[4]

Language and Expression

As we have seen, Gramsci is associated with a number of key terms of Marxist theory. "Hegemony" is one obvious example. While Gramsci didn't invent this word, he certainly developed it in important ways.

Additionally, many of the terms he used to help explain hegemony are also still important today. Examples of these include "coercion" and "consent," which describe how the ruling class maintains hegemony; and the "crisis of hegemony," or the moment when the ruling class can no longer convince people that society is set up as well as it could be.

An interesting discussion about the language of the text is whether or not Gramsci used code words and code names to confuse his fascist jailors. Some scholars argue, for example, that "the philosophy of praxis" refers to Marxism, and that Karl Marx is "the founder of the philosophy of praxis." Similarly, Vladimir Lenin is either "Ilich" or "the greatest modern theoretician of the philosophy of praxis."[5]

Not all scholars are convinced of this, however. Some say instead that Gramsci is quite open with the use of Marxist language in the *Notebooks*. That said, it is true that Gramsci was not allowed to read much of what he would have liked while in prison, and that his letters and notes were carefully monitored.

NOTES

1   Alberto Burgio, *Per Gramsci: Crisi e potenza del moderno* (Roma: Derive Approdi, 2007), 49.

2   Benedetto Fontana, "Hegemony and Power in Gramsci," in *Hegemony: Studies in Consensus and Coercion*, ed. Richard Howson and Kylie Smith (New York: Routledge, 2008), 82.

3   Perry Anderson, "The Antinomies of Antonio Gramsci," *New Left Review* 100 (1976): 44.

4   Antonio Gramsci, *Quaderni del carcere*, ed. Felice Platone (Torino: Einaudi, 1948–51), Q. 19, 2010–11.

5   Antonio Gramsci, *Selections from the Prison Notebooks*, ed. Quintin Hoare and Geoffrey N. Smith (London: Lawrence & Wishart, 1971), x–xi.

MODULE 6
SECONDARY IDEAS

KEY POINTS

- Gramsci's most important secondary idea is his description of what will cause a crisis of hegemony.*

- Gramsci argues that there are two ways in which the ruling classes might try to prevent this crisis from resulting in a successful revolution: they would either turn to fascism,* or to the American model of capitalism.*

- Scholars today still use Gramsci's ideas to understand current economic crises, and can draw on them to consider the ways in which capitalism has developed throughout the world.

Other Ideas

While we have focused mostly on Antonio Gramsci's central idea of hegemony,* *Prison Notebooks* also includes a number of other significant points. It is worth examining further what he says about how a capitalist society will respond to a crisis of hegemony.

Gramsci argues that a crisis of hegemony occurs when the ruling class cannot provide "intellectual and moral leadership," and therefore loses control over a society. As Gramsci puts it in *Notebook* 7, "The old intellectual and moral leaders feel the ground slipping from under their feet; they perceive that their 'sermons' have become precisely mere 'sermons'."[1]

Though this makes it sound as if the "crisis" is one of belief, Gramsci assures readers that its roots are also economic.[2] More specifically, it is when a severe economic problem becomes a severe political problem that a crisis of hegemony is at hand.[3] However, Gramsci writes that

> **❝** It [hegemony] is the most purely political phase, and marks the decisive passage from the structure to the sphere of the complex superstructures; it is the phase in which previously germinated ideologies become 'party,' come into confrontation and conflict, until only one of them, or at least a single combination of them, tends to prevail, to gain the upper hand, to propagate itself throughout society— bringing about not only a unison of economic and political aims, but also intellectual and moral unity. **❞**
>
> Antonio Gramsci, *Selections from the Prison Notebooks*.

economic problems can only *potentially* become political; they do not automatically create a crisis of hegemony. In order for that to happen, people must unite and resist the existing social order.

Gramsci gives a specific example of a crisis of hegemony: the time following World War I,* which included the Great Depression.*⁴ According to Gramsci, during this period, "big masses [of people] suddenly passed from political passivity to a certain activity." This meant that suddenly, many people stopped supporting the ruling classes, and instead began to demand change. As disorganized as these people were, they had the potential to cause a revolution.⁵

Exploring the Ideas

Gramsci claims that the ruling classes have two ways to respond to a crisis of hegemony. First, they may implement a fascist system, a system of government based on a dictator, military strength, and a strong sense of nationalism.* Second, they may turn to the American model of capitalism, which was characterized by Fordism,* or the mass production of goods, and by paying workers just enough that they could buy the products they made.

Gramsci calls both of these "passive revolutions,"* since they are controlled by the ruling classes. While society may be partially reformed, it is not transformed.

Passive revolutions, in other words, are methods by which the ruling classes can maintain their hegemony. One way in which this works is by rebuilding the economic system so that it appears to address concerns while also continuing to support those in power. For example, the fascist system that rose in Italy included a planned economy,* which meant that the central government dictated how it should work. This allowed the dictator, Benito Mussolini,* to keep society structured in a way that benefited his political interests, and also those of large Italian corporations. Therefore, no real transformation took place.

The United States offers another, different, example of a passive revolution. During the early twentieth century, the mass production associated with Fordism increased profits for businesses. This allowed them to pay workers moderately more—enough, for instance, for them to buy the goods they were making. This satisfied many who had been disgruntled, and social unrest gradually faded.

Coercion* (force or the credible threat of force) and consent* play a key role in this process. Under fascism, the ruling class forces people—often violently—to obey rules. Under Fordism, people are persuaded to adopt specific habits, rituals, and ways of running their families that support the new economic system.

Overlooked

Traditionally, those who study *Prison Notebooks* focus on Gramsci's concept of hegemony, and also on his description of how capitalism works. This has led them to comment mostly on how Gramsci broke away from some of Marxism's* core principles, and not on the ways in which he further developed those principles.

However, this reading has recently been challenged by writers in Italy[6] and elsewhere.[7] These newer understandings emphasize the ways in which Gramsci developed Marxist ideas. This rereading of *Prison Notebooks* has helped to clarify Gramsci's meaning. For example, it helps us see that in Gramsci's theory, economic changes provide only the potential for political change—they do not guarantee it (as traditional Marxism claimed).

One aspect of the book that deserves further study is the way in which Gramsci links politics, economics, and culture. For example, he argues that a crisis of hegemony is a political and cultural crisis, but he also comments on the way it begins as an economic crisis. He discusses Marx's book *Capital*, an important work of economic theory, and discusses how declining profits can result in a crisis of hegemony.[8]

In the United States, Gramsci observed, declining profits led to the mass production associated with Fordism.[9] It might also be possible to argue that European countries adopted similar models of capitalism because they also faced declining profits, and the system in the United States seemed to provide an answer.[10] In this way, further study of Gramsci's *Notebooks* might help today's theorists better understand how capitalism has developed around the world.

NOTES

1 Gramsci, *Selections from the Prison Notebooks*, Q. 7. 242.

2 Antonio Gramsci, *Quaderni del carcere*. Edizione critica dell'Istituto Gramsci a cura di Valentino Gerratana (Torino: Einaudi, 2001), Q. 13, 1582.

3 Gramsci, *Quaderni*, Q. 10, 1279.

4 Gramsci, *Quaderni*, Q. 13, 1603.

5 Gramsci, *Quaderni*, Q. 13, 1603.

6 For example, Fabio Frosini and Guido Liguori, eds, *Le parole di Gramsci* (Roma: Carocci, 2004); Alberto Burgio, *Gramsci storico. Una lettura dei "Quaderni del Carcere"* (Roma: Laterza, 2003).

7   For example, Peter Thomas, *The Gramscian Moment: Philosophy, Hegemony and Marxism* (Leiden: Brill, 2009).

8   Gramsci, *Quaderni*, Q. 10, 1278.

9   Gramsci, *Quaderni*, Q. 10, 1313.

10 Gramsci, *Quaderni*, Q. 22, 2178–79.

MODULE 7
ACHIEVEMENT

KEY POINTS

- Gramsci's main achievement is his discussion of how hegemony* works, as well as the ideas that this discussion leads to (such as the idea of a crisis of hegemony*).

- Gramsci has also been recognized for the way he analyzes capitalism,* his descriptions of the economic problems caused by capitalism, and the advice he offers on how people can come together to resist it.

- *Prison Notebooks* draws on and develops the work of Karl Marx,* Vladimir Lenin,* and other Marxist* thinkers.

Assessing the Argument

As we have seen, one of the main questions Antonio Gramsci wants to answer in *Prison Notebooks* is that of "why, in spite of the serious economic crisis and of the apparently revolutionary situation in a large part of Western Europe … was it not possible to successfully repeat the victorious experience of the Bolsheviks* in Russia?"[1] That is, why did the Russian Revolution* occur, while other countries in Europe experienced no such uprising?

Gramsci's home country offers one example. Between 1919 and 1920, a socialist revolution seemed in the making in Italy. This time, known as the Biennio Rosso* (or red biennium), was marked by strikes, factory occupations, and guerilla warfare; however, it did not result in a socialist* society. Instead, it was brutally crushed during the rise of the fascist* dictator Benito Mussolini.* Gramsci wanted to address why the Biennio Rosso, and movements like it, had failed.

❝ The claim that every fluctuation of politics and ideology can be presented and expounded as an immediate expression of the structure [the base] must be contested in theory as primitive infantilism, and combated in practice with the authentic testimony of Marx, the author of concrete political and historical works.**❞**

Antonio Gramsci, *Selections from the Prison Notebooks*

This meant addressing a larger question: What political system would create a society in which nobody was exploited? As he put it, "what political theory can give expression to—and, importantly, shape and guide—the popular and subaltern* [low status] classes' attempts to awaken from the nightmares of their histories and to assume social and political leadership[?]"[2]

Gramsci answered these questions through analyzing capitalism and the economic problems it caused. He also gave advice for challenging capitalist systems. At the heart of this argument is his concept of hegemony, which helped him describe how those in power in capitalist societies maintained and exercised that power, as well as how they exploited working-class people.

Today, he is remembered both for his own innovative ideas and for the way he developed the ideas of important Marxists thinkers such as Vladimir Lenin and even Marx himself.

Achievement in Context

One of the reasons why Gramsci pursued the questions mentioned above is that he believed the Marxists of his day had not been able to satisfactorily answer them. The international organization known as the Second International,* for example, appeared not to have an answer for why the Russian Revolution succeeded while other revolutions had not. It had also been critiqued by important Marxists thinkers such as Vladimir Lenin, the revolutionary writer Leon Trotsky,* and the German socialist and writer Rosa Luxemburg.*

As these thinkers—and Gramsci too—saw it, the problem was that the Second International claimed that if the base* (everyday economic relationships) could be affected, then a culture's values and beliefs (its superstructure*) would automatically change as well. They called this kind of thinking "economic determinism"*—the idea that one thing will necessarily lead to another.

Gramsci's way of overcoming this problem was to develop the concept of hegemony to an extent that Marxist theory had not done before. This does not mean that he broke away from Marx's ideas; instead, he elaborated key parts of them. He was informed here by his reading of the Italian philosopher Benedetto Croce,* whose insights into culture helped Gramsci see the importance of a society's beliefs and values. Thus, he was able to show that culture and economics are linked in ways that traditional Marxism had not.

It is also important to remember that Gramsci does not write political and economic theory alone. He also discusses the practical solutions that Lenin had offered based on his experiences as a leader of the Russian Revolution.

Limitations

Prison Notebooks shows that societies can be understood by studying economics, politics, and culture. If this seems natural to us nowadays, it is in part because of Gramsci's work: his method now seems normal. Today, scholars have used this method to understand cultures and political systems throughout history.

That said, much of Gramsci's writing is aimed specifically at understanding how capitalism worked in the early twentieth century. In other words, he wanted to know about the specific kind of capitalism that developed after World War I* and the Great

Depression.* As he makes clear, capitalism and hegemony change and evolve throughout history, and it is important to know about the historical context in which economic and political systems exist.[3]

This also acts as a warning for scholars today. Gramsci's concepts may still apply to our current society, but we must also acknowledge that things have changed since the 1920s and 1930s. Therefore, those who study Gramsci must be careful not to "stretch" his ideas to explain circumstances for which they were not designed. However, we should not write them off as useless, either, as they may help us understand today's economic and social relationships.

NOTES

1   Carlos Nelson Coutinho, *Gramsci's Political Thought* (Leiden: Brill, 2012), 50.

2   Peter Thomas, *The Gramscian Moment: Philosophy, Hegemony and Marxism* (Leiden: Brill, 2009), 159.

3   Antonio Gramsci, *Quaderni del carcere*, Edizione critica dell'Istituto Gramsci a cura di Valentino Gerratana (Torino: Einaudi, 2001), Q. 17, 1949.

MODULE 8
PLACE IN THE AUTHOR'S WORK

KEY POINTS

- In his writing, Gramsci explored relationships between the systems that help society function: economics, culture, and government, for example. He also encourages workers to unite against the ruling class.*

- *Prison Notebooks* is Gramsci's most important text; it is remembered for the concepts it adds to Marxist* theory, and for the guidance it offers to the working classes.

- Although the *Notebooks* had no influence during Gramsci's lifetime, the text became extraordinarily important for political movements and for social scientists.

Positioning

Before *Prison Notebooks*, Antonio Gramsci's most important text was "Some Aspects of the Southern Question"—a piece he was still working on when he was arrested.[1] In it, he writes about power, social class, the divide between people who live in cities and people who live in rural areas, and international relations.

He is particularly concerned with how the bourgeoisie* (ruling classes) who lived in northern Italy relate to the proletariat* (industrial workers) and peasants* (agricultural workers), writing, "The Northern bourgeoisie has subjugated the South of Italy and the Islands, and reduced them to exploitable colonies." He further demonstrates how the bourgeoisie had convinced northern industrial workers that the agricultural workers of the south were "inferior beings, semi-barbarians, or total barbarians."[2]

It was important, Gramsci argued, for these working-class groups

> **❝** Revolutionaries see history as a creation of their own spirit, as being made up of a continuous series of violent tugs at the other forces of society—both active and passive, and they prepare the maximum of favourable conditions for the definitive tug (revolution). **❞**

Antonio Gramsci, *Selections from the Prison Notebooks*

to organize themselves into one powerful political group. Gramsci called on intellectuals who believed in Marxist principles to help educate and unite workers. As he puts it, "This is gigantic and difficult, but precisely worthy of every sacrifice on the part of those intellectuals—from North and South—who have understood that only two social forces are essentially national and bearers of the future: the proletariat and the peasants."[3]

We can see that even in this early text, Gramsci was beginning to think about the concept of hegemony* and the role that intellectuals would play in a revolution (what he called "organic intellectuals"*).

Integration

Though we have been discussing them as if they were a single text, readers should remember that Gramsci's 33 *Notebooks* are literally a collection of notes: they includes his ideas, reflections, translations, and writing about books that have influenced him.

Four of these *Notebooks* are devoted to translation, and 29 to reflection on theory. About half are "special" (Gramsci's own term) in that they deal with particular themes, and the rest are labeled "miscellaneous" and cover a range of material.

While this might sound chaotic, many Gramsci scholars have observed that the *Notebooks* come together well. One such scholar, Peter D. Thomas,* observes that the *Prison Notebooks* "have a fundamental coherence and respond to specific questions posed in a particular conjuncture."[4] Thomas is here referring to issues such as how the Russian Revolution* of 1917 had succeeded where others had not, and why the Second International's* Marxist theories had been incomplete.

Like Gramsci's writing before his arrest, *Prison Notebooks* deals with social relationships: economics, culture, power relations (the way that social power is distributed throughout a society), and so on. Also like his other work, it encourages factory workers and peasants to unite against capitalism.*

Additionally, all of Gramsci's writing should be considered against the backdrop of history. He was very much concerned with addressing the consequences of events such as the Russian Revolution, World War I,* the Great Depression,* the rise of fascism,* and the new forms of capitalism that developed in the United States (called Americanism*).

Significance

Prison Notebooks would never have been published were it not for Gramsci's sister-in-law, Tatiana Schucht.* She managed to smuggle the 33 notebooks out of Gramsci's room and send them to Moscow.

Parts of the *Notebooks* were published between 1948 and 1951[5] with the help of Palmiro Togliatti,* then leader of the Italian Communist Party (PCI).*[6] Gramsci died in 1937, so he was unable to witness the wave of interest triggered by his work.

Gramsci's work did not spread as quickly outside of Italy. This was in part because, as the US University of Notre Dame professor and Gramsci scholar Joseph A. Buttigieg* observes, Gramsci's work challenges the established ideas of Marxists such as Vladimir Lenin,* and Karl Marx* himself. It was also because his work was not translated into English until 1971, and the entire collection of notebooks was not published until 1976.[7]

However, in the late 1960s and early 1970s, a new generation of leftists and political activists "discovered" Gramsci's work. Since then, he has become increasingly well known. And while *Prison Notebooks* is considered the most important text Gramsci wrote, scholars today are beginning to study his other writings.

The growing body of scholarship on Gramsci's work indicates that he is more important today than at any other time in his life. As Buttigieg puts it, he is "ubiquitous in academic writings in a broad spectrum of fields ranging from cultural studies* and postcolonial* studies to education and anthropology."[8] Here, "cultural studies" examines how certain ideas and elements seemingly become "normal" within a certain society; postcolonial studies inquires into the various cultural and social legacies of colonialism (the occupation and exploitation of one land or people by another); while anthropology is the study of humankind, commonly culture, belief, and society.

NOTES

1   Carlos Nelson Coutinho, *Gramsci's Political Thought* (Leiden: Brill, 2012), 47.

2   Antonio Gramsci, "Some Aspects of the Southern Question," in Antonio Gramsci, *Selections from Political Writings, 1910–20*, ed. and trans. Quintin Hoare and John Mathews (London: Lawrence & Wishart, 1977), 441–63.

3   Coutinho, *Gramsci's Political Thought*, 47.

4   Peter Thomas, *The Gramscian Moment: Philosophy, Hegemony and Marxism* (Leiden: Brill, 2009), 46.

5   Antonio Gramsci, *Quaderni del carcere*, ed. Felice Platone (Torino: Einaudi, 1948–51).

6   Joseph Buttigieg, in Coutinho, *Gramsci's Political Thought*, x.

7   Antonio Gramsci, *Quaderni del carcere*, Edizione critica a cura di Valentino Gerratana (Torino: Einaudi, 1976).

8   Buttigieg, in Coutinho *Gramsci's Political Thought*, xi.

SECTION 3
IMPACT

MODULE 9
THE FIRST RESPONSES

KEY POINTS

- Those who encountered Gramsci's work when it was originally published responded most to his deep understanding of the ideas of Karl Marx* and Vladimir Lenin,* and also to the way he addressed historical events, such as the Russian Revolution* of 1917.

- The most important critique of *Prison Notebooks* is that it was a product of its time and place, and is therefore not relevant today.

- Others have responded that Gramsci's ideas about hegemony,* coercion,* and consent* are still crucial for understanding capitalism* today.

Criticism

Antonio Gramsci was only 46 when he died in Rome in 1937, more than 10 years before his *Prison Notebooks* was published in his home country of Italy (as *Quaderni del carcere*). It was not until 1971 that it appeared in English, making it far more accessible to scholars. As a consequence, he was not alive for any of the academic debate that surrounded his work.

However, once scholars became acquainted with Gramsci's writing, they discussed and debated it a great deal. The best-known critique comes from three political science professors: Peter Burnham,* Randall Germain,* and Michael Kenny.* They argue that *Prison Notebooks* should be seen as a product of the time and place in which it was written: Italy in the 1920s and 1930s. It would be a mistake, they claim, to assign the text too much contemporary relevance.[1]

> **66** What we can do, for the moment, is to fix two major superstructural levels: the one that can be called 'civil society,' that is the ensemble of organisms commonly called 'private,' and that of 'political society' or 'the state.' These two levels correspond on the one hand to the function of 'hegemony' which the dominant group exercises throughout society, and on the other hand to that of 'direct domination' or command exercises through the state and 'juridical' government. **99**
>
> Antonio Gramsci, *Selections from the Prison Notebooks*

Other scholars have criticized more specific elements of Gramsci's work. Some, like the Marxist* scholar Perry Anderson,* have pointed toward contradictions in his theories. However, such arguments have not affected Gramsci's importance today. In fact, they may even have made him more significant, since they contribute to discussions about him.

Responses

The renowned Marxist and Gramscian scholar Carlos Coutinho* of Brazil has offered a response to Burnham, Germain, and Kenny's critique that *Prison Notebooks* is relevant only to the time and place in which it was written. Coutinho argues that Gramsci's ideas are as important as ever, and he gives as an example a new school of thought emerging among those who study international relations.

This perspective, referred to as neo-Gramscian,* was begun by Robert Cox,* emeritus professor at York University. In his article "Gramsci, Hegemony and International Relations: An Essay in Method" (1983), he argues that capitalism has emerged as an international system, and that a global ruling class* exercises control of people across societies through coercion and consent.

Cox believes that Gramsci's work can help scholars understand how international relationships and economic systems have come into being and evolved.[2] Additionally, he and other neo-Gramscians argue that it is important to see that our world is organized by social classes, not just by states.

Conflict and Consensus

Gramsci's ideas have come to influence nearly every social science discipline. Today, the Gramsci scholar Joseph A. Buttigieg* notes, "Gramsci has become a 'classic' that demands to be read."[3] Gramsci's ideas have also been important influences for left-wing political groups around the world. Many of their strategies and practices have been shaped by his work.

However, it is not only Marxist intellectuals and leftists who are interested in Gramsci. Recently, even conservatives have read his work. Somewhat surprisingly, their reaction has not always been negative. In April 2007, Nicolas Sarkozy,* the former French president and leader of the conservative Union for a Popular Movement (UMP)* party, admitted, "In the end, I have made Gramsci's analysis mine: power is gained through ideas."[4] Similarly, Michael Gove,* the United Kingdom's former minister for education in the Conservative* government, drew on Gramsci when he argued that education could be a tool that not only supported inequality, but made it look normal.[5]

That said, it is important to remember that reading Gramsci is not easy. His writing is complex, and *Prison Notebooks* was left unfinished. There is a danger in reading Gramsci carelessly: it is easy to misunderstand his arguments, and therefore to see them as something other than a call for revolution. As the philosophy professor Alberto Burgio* recently put it, *Prison Notebooks* is often used as a "supermarket for ideas."[6]

NOTES

1   Peter Burnham, "Neo-Gramscian Hegemony and the International Order," *Capital & Class* 15, no. 3 (1991); Randall D. Germain and Michael Kenny, "Engaging Gramsci: International Relations Theory and the New Gramscians," *Review of International Studies* 24, no. 1 (1998).

2   Robert Cox, "Social Forces, States and World Orders: Beyond International Relations Theory," *Millennium – Journal of International Studies* 10, no. 2 (1981): 126–55.

3   Joseph Buttigieg, in Adam David Morton, *Unravelling Gramsci: Hegemony and Passive Revolution in the Global Political Economy* (London: Pluto Press, 2007), ix.

4   Nicolas Sarkozy, *Le Figaro* (April 17, 2007); also quoted in the French edition of *Le Monde Diplomatique* (July 2012), accessed February 26, 2016, www.monde-diplomatique.fr/2012/07/KEUCHEYAN/47970#nb2.

5   "Michael Gove Speaks About the Importance of Teaching," GOV.UK, accessed April 30, 2014, www.gov.uk/government/speeches/michael-gove-speaks-about-the-importance-of-teaching.

6   Alberto Burgio, "Lezioni Gramsciane," *Il Manifesto*, January 10, 2010.

THE EVOLVING DEBATE

KEY POINTS

- Gramsci's *Prison Notebooks* has been particularly important for Marxist* intellectuals and left-wing political groups.

- Gramsci's ideas have given rise to the school of thought in international relations and political economy (a field that combines politics, law, and economics) known as neo-Gramscianism.*

- Gramsci has also influenced academic fields such as cultural studies,* which examines how certain ideas and factors come to seem "normal" within a certain culture; postcolonialism,* the study of the legacies of colonialism; and subaltern studies,* learning about how certain groups of people have traditionally suffered oppression because of aspects such as their race, gender, class, or sexual preference.

Uses and Problems

Since it was published in Italy in 1948, Antonio Gramsci's *Prison Notebooks* has inspired a great deal of popular and academic debate. As Joseph Buttigieg,* professor of English at the University of Notre Dame, remarks, "Within the space of a few years, hundreds of articles and books were written explicating, analysing and debating Gramsci's concept[s]."[1]

In particular, Gramsci's concept of hegemony* has helped rejuvenate Marxism. For example, a new generation of Marxists took up Gramsci's thinking in the 1960s and 1970s. These included the French Marxist philosopher Louis Althusser,* the history and

> **❝I** found that Gramsci's thinking was helpful in understanding the meaning of international organization with which I was principally concerned. Particularly valuable was his concept of hegemony, but valuable also were several related concepts which he had worked out for himself or developed from others.**❞**
>
> Robert Cox, "Gramsci, Hegemony and International Relations: An Essay in Method"

sociology* professor Perry Anderson,* and the Greek Marxist and writer Nicos Poulantzas.*

Gramsci has also helped shape political movements begun in places such as Brazil, where people have come together to resist imperialism* (where one country controls another country by means such as economics or military force).[2]

Even after the fall of the Soviet Union* in 1991, interest in Gramsci remained strong.[3] This is because his ideas seem relevant to many of the subjects that have interested people over the past several decades. Issues such as how wealth should be distributed, what types of sexuality should be allowed, and the Great Recession* can all be discussed using Gramsci's theories.

Schools of Thought

Although Gramsci's ideas are relevant to many academic disciplines, they have been most useful to those who study international relations and political economy (a field that combines politics, law, and economics). Those who draw significantly on Gramsci's perspective are known as neo-Gramscians.

Neo-Gramscians explore how the world is shaped by ideas, institutions, and resources; they are particularly interested in how control of these factors is associated with power. Neo-Gramscianism is distinct in how it focuses on worldwide economic and political developments, and class interests.

Another important element of this perspective is that in today's world, hegemony exists not because of individual countries; instead, neo-Gramscians focus on the state-society complex,* or a collection of ideas and economic relations that affect many countries.[4] As international relations professor Henk Overbeek* puts it, "Hegemony in the global system is … a form of class rule, and not primarily a relationship between states."[5]

The origins of neo-Gramscianism are commonly traced to the British political economist Robert Cox,* who published a number of foundational articles in the 1980s challenging the mainstream approaches in international relations and political economy.[6] Other important contributors to this field include Mark Rupert,* professor of political science at Syracuse University; Stephen Gill,* the distinguished research professor of political science at York University; the so-called "Amsterdam School of International Relations;"*[7] and a number of independent researchers, such as Andreas Bieler* and Adam David Morton.*

In Current Scholarship

One recent and significant work of Gramscian scholarship is the *Gramscian Dictionary* (*Dizionario Gramsciano* in Italian), a 900-page volume with more than 600 entries.[8] This reference guide shows the strength of interest in Gramsci's work, and that there is plenty of need for a deeper understanding of his writing.

This text attempts to demonstrate that Gramsci's 33 *Prison Notebooks* cohere. This is important because previous readings of Gramsci, sometimes intentionally and sometimes unintentionally, leave out important ideas or themes. The dictionary addresses this by taking into account the entirety of Gramsci's original text.

Additionally, important books of philosophy and political theory by, among others, Italian professor of philosophy Fabio Frosini,* professor of politics and history Peter Thomas,* and professor of political theory Carlos Nelson Coutinho* have helped to clarify Gramsci's philosophy and ideas.[9] These works have also explored new ways to understand Karl Marx.*

Still other scholars have tried to show how it can be useful to apply Gramsci's ideas to today's world. For example, the professor of philosophy and communications Alberto Burgio's* latest book, *Senza Democrazia (Without Democracy)*,[10] examines the historical and political developments from the 1980s through to the Great Recession.[11] Another is Adam David Morton's study of the *Notebooks*, which looks at how countries have contributed to and affected world economic and cultural relations.

NOTES

1 Joseph Buttigieg, in Adam D. Morton, *Unravelling Gramsci: Hegemony and Passive Revolution in the Global Political Economy* (London: Pluto Press, 2007), viii.

2 On the influence of Gramsci's thought on the development of Marxism in post-World War II Brazil, see Carlos Coutinho, *Gramsci's Political Thought* (Leiden: Brill, 2012), 163–88.

3 Buttigieg, in Morton, *Unravelling Gramsci*, ix; Marcus E. Green, ed., *Rethinking Gramsci* (New York: Routledge, 2011), 2.

4 Henk Overbeek, "Transnational Class Formation and Concepts of Control: Towards a Genealogy of the Amsterdam Project in International Political Economy," *Journal of International Relations and Development* 7, no. 2 (2004): 126.

5 Overbeek, "Transnational Class Formation," 127.

6 Robert W. Cox, "Social Forces, States and World Orders: Beyond International Relations Theory," *Millennium – Journal of International Studies* 10, no. 2 (1981): 126–55; Robert W. Cox, "Gramsci, Hegemony and International Relations: An Essay in Method," *Millennium – Journal of International Studies* 12, no. 2 (1983): 162–75; and Robert W. Cox, *Production, Power and World Order: Social Forces in the Making of History*

(New York: Columbia University Press, 1987).

7   An important work produced within the Amsterdam School is Kees van der Pijl, *The Making of an Atlantic Ruling Class* (London: Verso, 1984); an overview is provided by Overbeek, "Transnational Class Formation."

8   Guido Liguori and Pasquale Voza, eds, *Dizionario Gramsciano* (Roma: Carocci, 2009).

9   Peter Thomas, *The Gramscian Moment: Philosophy, Hegemony and Marxism* (Leiden: Brill, 2009); Fabio Frosini, *Gramsci e la filosofia. Saggio sui "Quaderni del carcere"* (Roma: Carocci, 2003); Carlos Nelson Coutinho, *Gramsci's Political Thought* (Leiden: Brill, 2012).

10 Alberto Burgio, *Senza Democrazia* (Roma: Derive Approdi, 2009).

11 Alberto Burgio, *Gramsci storico. Una lettura dei "Quaderni del carcere"* (Roma: Editori Laterza, 2003).

MODULE 11
IMPACT AND INFLUENCE TODAY

KEY POINTS

- Those who have studied Gramsci's *Prison Notebooks* have used it to help explain today's political, economic, and social developments; examples of these include the Great Recession* and the protests and uprisings known as the Arab Spring.*

- Gramsci's reading of Karl Marx* and Vladimir Lenin* has helped rejuvenate Marxist* discussion and theory.

- In the field of international relations, scholars use Gramsci's insights to challenge traditional perspectives.

Position

Because the text of Antonio Gramsci's *Prison Notebooks* is compiled from separate notebooks, and because it is unfinished, it has been the subject of a range of interpretations.

The earliest Gramsci scholars, working in the middle of the twentieth century, focused mostly on his central idea, hegemony,* as well as on how this played out in Italy in the form of the struggle between the working classes and ruling classes.*

More recently, scholars such as Alberto Burgio* and Fabio Frosini* have studied a whole range of subjects from *Prison Notebooks*, such as how it expands upon traditional Marxist ideas.[1] This sort of work led to the massive—and massively important—*Gramscian Dictionary* (2009), to which a number of Gramsci scholars contributed.[2]

The work of Perry Anderson* and Robert Cox* is also worthy of note. Anderson studied the ways in which politicians

❝ The crisis consists precisely in the fact that the old is dying and the new cannot be born; in this interregnum a great variety of morbid symptoms appear. ❞

Antonio Gramsci, *Selections from the Prison Notebooks*

have used ambiguous passages in *Prison Notebooks* to promote their agendas.[3] Cox began an entirely new perspective within the field of international relations based on Gramsci's ideas (neo-Gramscianism*).

These new insights into Gramsci's writing have also led to new ways of seeing today's world. For example, Gramsci's ideas can help us understand and analyze such important developments as the Great Recession[4] and the Arab Spring, a series of popular uprisings that began in the Arab world in 2010.[5]

Interaction

Most social sciences disciplines today include scholars who have drawn on Gramsci. His ideas helped open new lines of discussion and offered solutions to today's problems.

Gramsci's reading of Marx and Lenin has inspired new generations of Marxists. For example, his "philosophy of praxis,"* the idea that economics and culture must be seen as related, offers new ways of analyzing political and economic systems.

Additionally, Gramsci's concept of hegemony and his analysis of the state shaped many of the most important debates of the 1970s. These controversies focused on how capitalism* works, how power is distributed in capitalist societies, and how cultural values are formed.[6]

In the field of international relations, the neo-Gramscians have challenged two established perspectives. One is realism,* which assumes that the highest authorities are states, and that states try to gain power and stay secure. The other is liberalism,* which argues that states can find a way to live peacefully and cooperatively.

In fact, neo-Gramscian analysis has been called "perhaps the most important alternative to realist and liberal perspectives in the field."[7] Robert Cox, the original neo-Gramscian scholar, has explained that this approach is helpful in understanding how power relations in international society came to be, and how they have been shaped.[8]

Finally, Gramsci's writing has influenced current political movements, such as the Italian Communist Party (PCI)* and "Eurocommunism"* (which focuses intensely on how hegemony is maintained through culture). Readers should note, however, that it is now widely acknowledged that political leaders have sometimes used a biased reading of Gramsci's ideas to support their own political agendas.[9]

The Continuing Debate

Gramsci has figured prominently in the discussion of power today. For example, the French philosopher Michel Foucault* drew extensively on Gramsci in his writing on how power works and how it is exercised.[10] One difference between Foucault's and Gramsci's understandings of power is that for Gramsci, it is clearly the ruling class that exercises and maintains power,[11] while Foucault is less specific (something for which he has been criticized).

Gramsci is sometimes critiqued in debates about power, too—though even those who critique him rely on his ideas. For example, in *Reading Capital*, the French Marxist philosopher Louis Althusser* argues that Gramsci gives human action too much credit for shaping history,[12] though Althusser's work is at its root founded upon Gramsci's understanding of culture and power.[13]

In international relations, Gramsci's work, and the work of neo-Gramscians in turn, has sometimes been dismissed as too Marxist. However, some of its insights have entered mainstream thought. In realism, for example, scholars in the 1980s and 1990s developed hegemonic stability theory,* which suggests that one powerful nation can lead to greater international stability. While such a theory runs counter to much of Gramsci's thinking, it nevertheless draws on some of his concepts.[14]

Similarly, the international relations professor Joseph Nye* has written about "soft power," or power that comes through (for example) cultural influence, rather than through military force. This concept draws on Gramsci's understanding of how power is maintained and exercised through culture.[15]

NOTES

1 Alberto Burgio, *Gramsci storico. Una lettura dei "Quaderni del carcere"* (Roma: Laterza, 2003); Fabio Frosini and Guido Liguori, eds, *Le parole di Gramsci* (Roma: Carocci editore, 2004).

2 Guido Liguori and Pasquale Voza, eds, *Dizionario Gramsciano* (Roma: Carocci, 2009).

3 See Perry Anderson, "The Antinomies of Antonio Gramsci," *New Left Review* 100 (1976): 5–78.

4 See for example, Stathis Kouvelakis, "The Greek Cauldron," *New Left Review* 72 (2011).

5 See for example, Mohamed Rasha "Springtime for Marxism? The Possible Applications of Marxist Theory to the Events of the Arab Spring," *Social & Political Review* XXII (2012).

6 Bob Jessop, "Bringing the State Back in (Yet Again)," *International Review of Sociology: Revue Internationale de Sociologie* 11, no. 2 (2001): 149–73.

7 Michael G. Schechter, "Critiques of Coxian Theory: Background to a Conversation," in *The Political Economy of a Plural World: Critical Reflections on Power, Morals and Civilization*, ed. Robert W. Cox and Michael G. Schecter (London: Routledge, 2002), 2.

8 Robert Cox, "Social Forces, States and World Orders: Beyond International Relations Theory," *Millennium – Journal of International Studies* 10, no. 2 (1981): 126–55.

9   Chantal Mouffe and Anne Showstack Sassoon, "Gramsci in France and Italy: A Review of the Literature," *Economy and Society* 6, no. 1 (1977): 32.

10 Michel Foucault's conceptualization of power can be found in his *History of Sexuality, Volume One: The Will To Knowledge* (London: Penguin, 1998).

11 Alberto Burgio, *Per Gramsci: Crisi e potenza del moderno* (Roma: Derive Approdi, 2007), 136.

12 Louis Althusser and Etienne Balibar, *Reading Capital* (New York: Pantheon Books, 1971).

13 Louis Althusser, *For Marx* (London: Verso, 2005).

14 This theory is associated with and explained by Robert Gilpin in *The Political Economy of International Relations* (Princeton, NJ: Princeton University Press, 1987).

15 Joseph Nye, *Bound to Lead: The Changing Nature of American Power* (New York: Basic Books, 1990).

WHERE NEXT?

KEY POINTS

- Today, many disciplines draw on Gramsci's *Prison Notebooks.*

- Gramsci's ideas about power and hegemony* have influenced both Marxist* and non-Marxist scholars.

- Gramsci's insights on capitalism* and the problems it causes have been important in discussions about how to combat oppression.

Potential

One way to measure Antonio Gramsci's lasting importance, to which his *Prison Notebooks* notably contributes, is to consider how many times he has been referenced in the writing of others. As of 2014, the online Gramsci bibliography includes more than 19,000 texts written in 41 languages. These texts come from a range of backgrounds and theoretical approaches.[1] This volume of work is perhaps best described by the philosophy professor Fabio Frosini's* phrase, "world-wide *Gramsci renaissance.*"[2]

This is even more remarkable when we consider that it is only recently that scholars outside of Italy have begun to study *Prison Notebooks.* This has led to productive new discussions and perspectives. For example, one reviewer of the British scholar Peter Thomas's* recent book, *The Gramscian Moment,* commented that it "addresses" and "confronts" major figures in the field of international relations.[3] And as we have seen, neo-Gramscian* thought has challenged traditional perspectives in this field, such as realism* (the idea that international relations are shaped by individual countries, and that

> **❝ A 'crisis of authority' is spoken of: this is precisely the crisis of hegemony, or general crisis of the state. ❞**
> Antonio Gramsci, *Selections from the Prison Notebooks*.

these countries' primary goals are survival and the accumulation of power) and liberalism* (the idea that peace and cooperation between nations is possible).

Future Directions

Many of the problems Gramsci touches on in *Prison Notebooks* still plague the world today, though they may have taken on new forms. For example, countries around the globe are struggling to recover from the "Great Recession."* Many have argued that the Great Recession is the result of a crisis of hegemony,* which is much the same thing as Gramsci argued about the Great Depression* of the 1930s. Given that both events occurred under capitalist economic systems, Gramsci's analysis of capitalism can still be informative.

Gramsci's argument about how capitalism will respond to a crisis of hegemony is also still relevant. He warned that rearranging the social order to pacify protestors—what he called a passive revolution*—does not amount to a transformation of society. This idea might be useful in explaining why, recently, a number of right-wing movements have emerged to argue that the social order should not be rearranged. Examples include the Tea Party* movement in the United States, which demands a smaller and less influential government, and the Front National* in France, which calls for the sort of strict social policies that Gramsci argued were meant to support the established social arrangement.

However, the question of how an alternative version of society might be constructed, in which all people are free from oppression, is still open today. This alone seems to suggest that

Prison Notebooks is still as relevant now as it was when first written almost 80 years ago.

Summary

Prison Notebooks is widely seen as one of the most important texts in the social sciences. It has also had an important influence on political and social movements throughout the world.

Gramsci wrote the text in Italy between 1929 and 1935, after having been arrested for opposing the fascist* dictator Benito Mussolini.* Gramsci died before finishing it, leaving behind more than 2,300 pages (in 33 *Notebooks*). His book was eventually published in Italy in 1948, and was then translated into English in 1971.

In *Prison Notebooks*, Gramsci explains why Russia experienced a successful revolution in 1917 while, during the same time, socialist* revolutions did not succeed in Italy and elsewhere in Western Europe. He also provides guidance for industrial workers and peasants* on how to come together to resist the bourgeoisie.*

In focusing on the relationship between economics and culture, Gramsci expanded upon the theories of Karl Marx.* In turn, his thinking has been key for many Marxists who followed him, including Louis Althusser* and Perry Anderson.* Even non-Marxists have adopted his concepts of power and hegemony, which demonstrates how significant they are to today's discussion.

Finally, Gramsci's work remains relevant to our world today. As the Great Recession shows, our economic system still has problems, and those who believe in alternatives will likely continue to learn from Gramsci's ideas.

NOTES

1   This bibliography, which is regularly updated, can be found at: Fondazione Istituto Gramsci, "Bibliografia Gramsciana," accessed April 30, 2014, www. fondazionegramsci.org.

2   Fabio Frosini, quoted in Marcus E. Green, "Introduction: Rethinking Marxism and Rethinking Gramsci," in *Rethinking Gramsci* (New York: Routledge, 2011), 2.

3   Antonio Negri, "Reading Gramsci Anew. Review of Peter Thomas, The Gramscian Moment," *Historical Materialism* (2011), accessed February 22, 2016, www.historicalmaterialism.org/journal/online-articles/reading-gramsci-anew.

GLOSSARIES

GLOSSARY OF TERMS

Americanism: the model of capitalism specific to the United States when Gramsci wrote *Prison Notebooks*.

Amsterdam School of International Relations: those who work in international relations at the University of Amsterdam.

Arab Spring: the name given to the series of protests that have taken place in the Middle East and North Africa since 2010.

***Avanti!*:** meaning "forward" in English, this was the official daily newspaper of the Italian Socialist Party.

Base: a Marxist term for everyday economic developments and transactions.

Biennio Rosso: meaning "red biennium" (a biennium is two years) in English, this refers to the period of revolutionary upheaval in Italy between 1919 and 1920. This time was marked by mass strikes, land and factory occupations, and guerilla warfare. It was brutally crushed by the fascist militia led by Benito Mussolini.

Bolsheviks: a Russian political action group primarily comprised of urban workers, who would play a major role in the 1917 Revolution and go on to form the majority of the government of the Soviet Union in 1922

Bourgeoisie: in Marxist theory, the ruling classes or those who control a society's resources and production of goods and services.

Capitalism: an economic system that emphasizes the private ownership of land, natural resources, and technology, and the production of goods and services for profit.

Civil society: those organizations and institutions commonly associated with the "private" sphere of life, the family, Church, and so on.

Coercion: a term used by Gramsci to mean the threat of force. This is one way in which a ruling class can control others in society.

Common sense: according to Gramsci, ruling classes seek to convince others in society that the way things are is natural and normal—"common sense."

Communism: a political system proposed by Karl Marx in which workers own and manage resources and production. Under this system, the state and social classes cease to exist.

Consent: the term used by Gramsci to mean that the ruling classes manipulate ideas, beliefs, and values to get people to accept that the current social arrangement benefits them. This is one way in which a ruling class can control others in society.

Conservative Party: a British right-wing political party, founded in 1834.

Crisis of hegemony: a situation described by Gramsci in which economic problems cause people to lose faith in their leaders.

Cultural studies: a field of study focusing on understanding how certain ideas and facets come to seem "normal" within a given society.

Economic determinism: the traditional Marxist belief that developments in the economy (known as the "base") directly and automatically influence developments in the political, cultural, and ideological arena (the "superstructure").

Eurocommunism: the strategy adopted by European communist parties in the 1970s and 1980s, which focused intensely on how hegemony is maintained through culture.

Factory council movements: movements of Italian workers between 1919 and 1922 that defended the interests of labor against the ruling classes.

Fascism: a system of government that emphasizes extreme nationalism, military strength, and aggression, and gives a dictator extreme power to enforce order and national unity. Nazi Germany is a classic example of a fascist state.

Fordism: an economic system based on mass production. The word comes from the way the Ford Motor Company manufactured cars at the beginning of the twentieth century, which involved assembly lines, workers specializing in a single task, and maximizing efficiency.

Front National: a far-right party in France formerly led by Jean-Marie Le Pen and currently presided over by his daughter, Marine Le Pen.

Great Depression: the longest, deepest, and most widespread economic crisis of the twentieth century. It began with the collapse of the US stock market on October 29, 1929, and continued into the early 1940s. It was defined by unemployment, poor standards of living, decreased production and trade, and public anger against capitalism.

Great Recession: a term used to describe the severe economic downturn in world markets that began with the collapse of the US housing market in 2007.

Il Grido de Popolo: the former weekly newspaper of the Italian Socialist Party.

Hegemonic stability theory: a theory in the field of international relations which claims that one dominant nation-state in the international system leads to greater stability.

Hegemony: how ruling classes in a society gain, keep, and manage their power. Gramsci argued that the ruling classes maintain hegemony both economically and ideologically (that is, through ideas).

Historical materialism: the study of how economics shapes politics and societies.

Historiography: the writing of history, and the idea that history is ever-evolving.

Imperialism: when one country controls another through force or through political and economic domination.

Integral state: a Gramscian term which means that the ruling classes depend on a combination of political society (the police, the army, the courts, etc.) and civil society (the family, the education system, the Church, etc.) to attain and maintain hegemony.

Italian Communist Party (PCI): party cofounded by Gramsci, which split from the Italian Socialist Party in 1921. Although it was outlawed by the fascist regime of Benito Mussolini, it played a major role in the Italian resistance movement.

Italian Socialist Party (PSI): a leftist party that existed in Italy between 1892 and 1994.

Liberalism (or liberal internationalism): a school of international relations theory that suggests states can, and ultimately will, achieve peace and mutual cooperation.

Marxism: the name ascribed to the political and economic philosophy of Karl Marx. It emphasized an end to private ownership of resources and property. Instead, these would be controlled by the working classes.

Means of production: a term referring to the resources and technology necessary to make goods and services.

Nationalism: extreme loyalty toward one's country.

Neo-Gramscianism: an approach to social analysis which asserts that a transnational ruling class has emerged and controls many societies worldwide through coercion and consent. Furthermore, it suggests that the world is organized by social class, and not by countries. This perspective begins with the work of scholar Robert Cox.

L'Ordine Nuovo: a weekly socialist newspaper cofounded by Antonio Gramsci in Italy that existed from 1919 to 1925.

Organic intellectual: an intellectual who helps organize people in order to challenge the hegemony of the ruling classes. Martin Luther King could arguably fit this mold, as he mobilized the masses against racial segregation in the United States.

Passive revolution: a Gramscian term that refers to societal change whereby the social order is rearranged to pacify protestors, but is not transformed.

Peasants: agricultural laborers.

Philosophy of praxis: for Gramsci, a theory which emphasizes that economics and culture must be seen as related in order to understand how the ruling class exerts control over workers.

Planned economy: an economic system that is dictated by a central government.

Postcolonial studies: the study of the relationships between European countries and the places they colonized, as well as the consequences for people who lived—and live—in those places.

Proletariat: a term used by Marxists to refer to the collectivity of the working class.

Realism: a school of international relations theory that assumes the following: that states are the primary actors in the world; that states all share the goal of survival; that states provide for their own security.

Revolutionary workers movement: the revolutionary movement of Italian industrial workers that tried to overthrow the established order and implement socialism/communism.

Ruling class: the class of people in a given society that exerts power and authority (also called the bourgeoisie).

Russian Revolution: the name used for the two revolutions that occurred in Russia in 1917, leading to the collapse of Tsarist rule and the eventual establishment of the Soviet Union in 1922 after a period of civil war. The first, in March, led to the resignation of Nicolas II; in the second, in October, the communist Bolsheviks, led by Vladimir Lenin, overthrew the Provisional Government to take power.

Second International: an international organization of Marxist groups that formed following the death of Karl Marx in 1883 and existed until 1916. It argued that the economic problems associated with advanced capitalist societies would ultimately lead to the establishment of socialism.

Socialism: a political and economic theory which advocates that resources and the production of goods and services should be owned and regulated by the community as a whole (and not by individual citizens).

Sociology: the study of society and social behavior.

Soviet Union (1922–91): a federation of communist republics in Asia and Europe that existed until 1991. Its capital city was Moscow, Russia. The Soviet Union was established after the Russian Revolution, and it was among the largest and most powerful countries in the world.

State-society complex: a perspective in political science which claims that it is social class, not individual states, that cause hegemony on an international level.

Subaltern: a term used to designate people of low status, without influence or "voice."

Subaltern studies: the study of how certain groups of people have traditionally suffered oppression because of (for example) their race, gender, class, or sexual preference.

Superstructure: a Marxist term that means the political, cultural, and social parts of a society.

Tea Party movement: a conservative political movement formed in 2009 in the United States that demands a significant reduction in the size and influence of the federal government.

Third International (Comintern): an international organization of communist parties that existed between 1919 and 1943. Its central aim was to promote an international working-class revolution.

Transnational capitalist class: a ruling class whose power extends beyond individual nations.

Tsar: the title given to the ruler of Russia (and its empire) from 1547 to 1917.

Union for a Popular Movement (UMP): known as the Union pour un Mouvement Populaire in French, a conservative political party founded in 2002 as a merger of different center-right parties. It was renamed and replaced in May 2015 by the Republicans (les Républicains).

War of maneuver: a term used by Gramsci that means a "frontal attack" by revolutionaries on organizations of state power (such as courts of law).

War of position: a term used by Gramsci that means to resist and change a society's culture, thereby preparing it to revolt against a ruling class.

World War I (1914–18): a global conflict fought between the Central Powers (Germany, Austria-Hungary, and the Ottoman Empire) and the victorious Allied Powers (United Kingdom, France, Russia, Italy and, after 1917, the United States). More than 16 million people would die as a result of the war.

World War II (1939–45): a global conflict fought between the Axis Powers (Germany, Italy, and Japan) and the victorious Allied Powers (United Kingdom and its commonwealth, the former Soviet Union, and the United States).

Workers' councils: councils consisting of both the employer and employees who together discuss and negotiate working conditions, wages, and so on.

PEOPLE MENTIONED IN THE TEXT

Louis Althusser (1918–90) was a French Marxist and professor of philosophy at the École Normale Supérieure in Paris. He is the author of *Reading Capital* (1968), among several other important works.

Perry Anderson (b. 1938) is professor of history and sociology at the University of California, Los Angeles, and a former editor of the *New Left Review*. He is the author of several important works, including *Lineages of the Absolutist State* (1974).

Aristotle (384–322 B.C.E.) was an Ancient Greek philosopher. He wrote on a wide range of subjects including ethics, physics, and politics. Aristotle is credited with being the first scientist in history and is the author of the foundational work *Politics*.

Andreas Bieler is professor of political economy at Nottingham University. He is the author of *The Struggle for a Social Europe: Trade Unions and EMU in Times of Global Restructuring* (2006), among other important publications.

Amadeo Bordiga (1889–1970) was an Italian Marxist and the cofounder, along with Antonio Gramsci, of the Italian Communist Party.

Alberto Burgio is professor of philosophy and communication studies at the University of Bologna. He is the author of several important works in Italian, including *Per Gramsci: Crisi e potenza del moderno* (2007).

Peter Burnham is professor of political science and international studies at the University of Birmingham. He is the author of "Neo-Gramscian Hegemony and the International Order," among several other important works.

Joseph Buttigieg is professor of English at the University of Notre Dame. He is the editor and translator of a three-volume critical edition of Gramsci's *Prison Notebooks*, published by Columbia University Press between 1992 and 2007.

Carlos Coutinho (b. 1943) is professor of political theory at the Federal University of Rio de Janeiro. He is the author of *Gramsci's Political Thought* (2012).

Robert Cox (b. 1926) is professor emeritus of political science and social and political thought at York University. He is widely regarded as the founder of neo-Gramscianism in international relations and is the author of "Gramsci, Hegemony and International Relations: An Essay in Method," among several other important works.

Benedetto Croce (1866–1952) was an Italian philosopher and liberal politician whose writings were strongly influenced by the philosophies of Hegel and Marx. He is the author of *Materialismo storico ed economia Marxistica* (1900) (*Historical Materialism and the Economics of Karl Marx*, 2004), among several other important works.

Michel Foucault (1926–84) was a French historian and philosopher and professor of the history of systems of thought at the Collège de France. He is the author of several important works, including *Discipline and Punish* (1975).

Fabio Frosini is professor of philosophy at the University of Urbino "Carlo Bo." He is a scholar of Antonio Gramsci and the author of *Gramsci e la filosofia. Saggio sui "Quaderni del carcere"* (2003).

Giovanni Gentile (1875–1944) was an Italian philosopher and a passionate supporter of fascism. Gentile described himself as "the philosopher of fascism" and he was the ghostwriter of *A Doctrine of Fascism* (1932; officially authored by Benito Mussolini).

Randall Germain is professor of political science at Carleton University, Ottawa. He is the author of several important works, including "Engaging Gramsci: International Relations Theory and the New Gramscians" (1998).

Stephen Gill (b. 1950) is distinguished research professor of political science at York University. He is the author of several important works, including *Gramsci, Historical Materialism and International Relations* (1993).

Michael Gove (b. 1967) is a British Member of Parliament for the Conservative Party, and has served as government chief whip, secretary of state for education, and lord chancellor.

Gennaro Gramsci was a socialist activist and the older brother of Antonio Gramsci. The two shared a room together at Dettori Lyceum (a secondary school) in Cagliari, Italy.

Georg Wilhelm Friedrich Hegel (1770–1831) was a German philosopher whose theories heavily influenced Karl Marx. He is the author of *The Phenomenology of the Spirit* (1807), among several other important works.

Eric Hobsbawm (1917–2012) was a well-known British Marxist historian. He is the author of *The Age of Revolution* (1962), among many other important works.

Michael Kenny is professor of politics at Queen Mary College, University of London. He is the author of several important works, including "Engaging Gramsci: International Relations Theory and the New Gramscians" (1998).

Antonio Labriola (1843–1904) was an Italian Marxist philosopher whose approach to Marxism was more critical and open-ended than what was typical in the Second International. He strongly influenced many Italian political theorists in the early twentieth century, including Croce and Gramsci.

Vladimir Lenin (1870–1924) was founder of the Russian Communist Party, leader of the Russian Revolution, and the first head of the Soviet Union.

Rosa Luxemburg (1871–1919) was a Marxist thinker and writer, and an important figure in the development of German socialist thought and practice. She was killed by the German authorities after her involvement in an attempted communist uprising. She is the author of *Die Akkumulation des Kapitals* (1913) (*The Accumulation of Capital*, 1951).

Karl Marx (1818–83) was a German philosopher, economist, historian, and sociologist, and is widely considered one of the most influential social scientists. He is the author of *The Communist Manifesto* (1848) and *Das Kapital* (1867).

Adam David Morton is professor of political economy at the University of Sydney. He is the author of several important works, including *Unravelling Gramsci: Hegemony and Passive Revolution in the Global Political Economy* (2007).

Benito Mussolini (1883–1945) was the leader of the National Fascist Party in Italy. He was prime minister (and dictator) of the country from 1922 to 1943.

Nicolas II (Nikolai Alexandrovich Romanov, 1868–1918) was tsar of Russia from 1894 to 1917. He was overthrown during the Russian Revolution of 1917 and executed the following year.

Joseph Nye (b. 1937) is distinguished service professor of international relations at Harvard University and cofounder of the international relations theory known as neoliberalism. Nye is the author of several important works, including *Bound to Lead: The Changing Nature of American Power* (1990).

Henk Overbeek is professor of international relations at the University of Amsterdam. He has written several important works, including "Transnational Class Formation and Concepts of Control: Towards a Genealogy of the Amsterdam Project in International Political Economy" (2004).

Nicos Poulantzas (1936–79) was a Greek Marxist and a leading advocate of Eurocommunism in the 1970s. His most famous works include *Classes in Contemporary Capitalism* (1975), *Political Power and Social Classes* (1978), and *State, Power, and Socialism* (1978).

Mark Rupert is professor of political science at Syracuse University. He is the author of *Producing Hegemony: the Politics of Mass Production and American Global Power* (1995), among other important works.

Nicolas Sarkozy (b. 1955) is the former minister of the interior and president of France. He is currently the chairman of the conservative political party known as the Republicans (Les Républicains), formerly called the UMP.

Tatiana Schucht was Antonio Gramsci's sister-in-law. She smuggled his 33 *Notebooks* from Italy to Moscow, where she gave them to Palmiro Togliatti, the secretary of the Italian Communist Party, who later published them.

Angelo Tasca (1892–1960) was an Italian Marxist and a founding member of the Italian Communist Party.

Umberto Terracini (1895–1983) was an Italian Marxist and a founding member of the Italian Communist Party.

Peter Thomas is senior lecturer (associate professor) in politics and history at Brunel University. He is the author of several important works, including *The Gramscian Moment: Philosophy, Hegemony and Marxism* (2009).

Palmiro Togliatti (1893–1964) was an Italian Marxist and a founding member of the Italian Communist Party. Following Gramsci's imprisonment, he became the party's leader, a position that he maintained until his death.

Leon Trotsky (1879–1940) was a Russian Marxist revolutionary and key leader in the Russian Revolution. He was excluded from the government that would eventually form, and he lived in exile before being assassinated in Mexico. He is the author of *The History of the Russian Revolution* (1932), among several other important works.

WORKS CITED

WORKS CITED

Ameriks, Karl. "The Legacy of Idealism in the Philosophy of Feuerbach, Marx, and Kierkegaard." In *The Cambridge Companion to German Idealism*, edited by Karl Ameriks, 258–82. Cambridge: Cambridge University Press, 2000.

Avineri, Shlomo. *Hegel's Theory of the Modern State*. Cambridge: Cambridge University Press, 1972.

Beiser, Frederick. "Dark Days: Anglophone Scholarship Since the 1960s." In *German Idealism: Contemporary Perspectives*, edited by Espen Hammer, 70–91. Abingdon: Routledge, 2007.

Berlin, Isaiah. *Four Essays on Liberty*. Oxford: Oxford University Press, 1969.

Bonsiepen, Wolfgang. "Erste Zeitgenössische Rezensionen der Phänomenologie des Geistes." *Hegel-Studien* 14 (1979): 9–38.

Brandom, Robert. *Tales of the Mighty Dead: Historical Essays in the Metaphysics of Intentionality*. London: Harvard University Press, 2002.

Engels, Friedrich. Preface to the third (1885) German edition of Karl Marx's *The Eighteenth Brumaire of Louis Bonaparte*. In *Karl Marx and Frederick Engels Selected Works*. Moscow: Progress Publishers, 1968. Accessed August 11, 2015, https://www.marxists.org/archive/marx/works/1885/prefaces/18th-brumaire.htm.

Fanon, Frantz. *Black Skin, White Masks*. Translated by Charles Lam Markmann. London: Pluto Press, 1986.

Forster, Michael N. *Hegel's Idea of a Phenomenology of Spirit*. Chicago: University of Chicago Press, 1998.

Fukuyama, Francis. *The End of History and the Last Man*. London: Penguin, 1992.

Fulda, Hans Friedrich. *Das Problem einer Einleitung in Hegels Wissenschaft der Logik*. Frankfurt am Main: Klostermann, 1965.

Harris, Henry Silton. *Hegel's Ladder*. 2 vols. Cambridge: Hackett, 1997.

Haym, Rudolf. *Hegel und seine Zeit*. Berlin: R. Gaertner, 1857.

Hegel, Georg Wilhelm Friedrich. *The Difference between Fichte's and Schelling's Systems of Philosophy*. Edited by Walter Cerf and H. S. Harris. Albany: State University of New York Press, 1988.

____. *Elements of the Philosophy of Right*. Translated by H. B. Nisbet and edited by Allen Wood. Cambridge: Cambridge University Press, 1991.

____. *Faith and Knowledge*. Edited by Walter Cerf and H. S. Harris. Albany: State University of New York Press, 1988.

____. *The Letters*. Translated by Clark Butler and Christiane Seiler. Bloomington: University of Indiana Press, 1984.

____. "On the Prospects for a Folk Religion." In *Three Essays, 1793–1795*, edited and translated by Peter Fuss and John Dobbins, 30–58. Notre Dame, Indiana: University of Notre Dame Press, 1984.

____. *Phenomenology of Spirit*. Translated by A. V. Miller. Oxford: Oxford University Press, 1977.

____. *The Science of Logic*. Translated by George Di Giovanni. Cambridge: Cambridge University Press, 2015.

____. *The Science of Logic: 1, Encyclopedia of the Philosophical Sciences*. Translated by William Wallace. US: Hythloday Press, 2014.

____. *System of Ethical Life*. Edited and translated by T. M. Knox. Albany: State University of New York Press, 1979.

Hobbes, Thomas. *Leviathan: Cambridge Texts in the History of Political Thought*. Edited by Richard Tuck. Cambridge; New York: Cambridge University Press, 1991.

Honneth, Axel. *The Struggle for Recognition*. Translated by Joel Anderson. Cambridge: Polity Press, 1995.

Houlgate, Stephen. *Hegel's "Phenomenology of Spirit": A Reader's Guide*. London & New York: Bloomsbury Publishing, 2013.

____. *The Opening of Hegel's Logic: From Being to Infinity*. West Lafayette, IN: Purdue University Press, 2006.

Hyppolite, Jean. *Genesis and Structure of Hegel's* Phenomenology of Spirit. Translated by Samuel Cherniak and John Heckman. Evanston: Northwestern University Press, 1974.

Kojève, Alexandre. *Introduction to the Reading of Hegel: Lectures on* Phenomenology of Spirit. Translated by James H. Nichols, Jr. New York: Basic Books, 1969.

Kreines, James. "Hegel's Metaphysics: Changing the Debate." *Philosophy Compass* 1.5 (2006): 466–80.

Lukács, George. *The Young Hegel*. Translated by Rodney Livingstone. London: Merlin Press, 1975.

Marx, Karl. *Critique of Hegel's "Philosophy of Right."* Edited by Joseph O'Malley. Cambridge: Cambridge University Press, 1977.

McDowell, John. *Having the World in View: Essays on Kant, Hegel, and Schelling*. London: Harvard University Press, 2009.

Nicolin, Gunther (editor). *Hegel in Berichten seiner Zeitgenossen*. Hamburg: Felix Meiner Verlag, 1970.

Nimbalkar, Namita. "John Locke on Personal Identity." *Mens Sana Monographs*. 9.1 (2011): 268–75.

Pinkard, Terry. *Hegel: A Biography*. Cambridge: Cambridge University Press, 2000.

Pippin, Robert B. *Hegel's Idealism: The Satisfactions of Self-Consciousness*. Cambridge: Cambridge University Press, 1989.

Popper, Karl. *The Open Society and Its Enemies, Vol. 2. The High Tide of Prophecy: Hegel, Marx, and the Aftermath*. London: Routledge, 1952.

Quante, Michael. *Hegel's Concept of Action*. Translated by Dean Moyar. Cambridge: Cambridge University Press, 2004.

Rawls, John. *A Theory of Justice*. Cambridge, MA: Harvard University Press, 1971.

Rorty, Richard. "The Historiography of Philosophy: Four Genres." In *Philosophy in History*, edited by Richard Rorty, J. B. Schneewind, and Quentin Skinner, 31–49. Cambridge: Cambridge University Press, 1984.

Sellars, Wilfrid. "Empiricism and the Philosophy of Mind." In *Minnesota Studies in the Philosophy of Science, Volume I: The Foundations of Science and the Concepts of Psychology and Psychoanalysis*, edited by Herbert Feigl and Michael Scriven, 253–329. Minneapolis: University of Minnesota Press, 1956.

Singer, Peter. *Hegel*. Oxford: Oxford University Press, 1983.

Strawson, Peter. *Bounds of Sense: An Essay on Kant's* Critique of Pure Reason. London: Methuen, 1966.

Taylor, Charles. *Hegel*. Cambridge: Cambridge University Press, 1975.

___. *Sources of the Self: The Making of the Modern Identity.* Cambridge, MA: Harvard University Press, 1989.

Theunissen, Michael. *Hegels Lehre Vom Absoluten Geist Als Theologisch-Politischer Traktat*. Berlin: de Gruyter, 1970.

Ugilt, Rasmus. *The Metaphysics of Terror: The Incoherent System of Contemporary Politics.* London & New York: Bloomsbury Academic, 2012.

THE MACAT LIBRARY
BY DISCIPLINE

AFRICANA STUDIES

Chinua Achebe's *An Image of Africa: Racism in Conrad's Heart of Darkness*
W. E. B. Du Bois's *The Souls of Black Folk*
Zora Neale Huston's *Characteristics of Negro Expression*
Martin Luther King Jr's *Why We Can't Wait*
Toni Morrison's *Playing in the Dark: Whiteness in the American Literary Imagination*

ANTHROPOLOGY

Arjun Appadurai's *Modernity at Large: Cultural Dimensions of Globalisation*
Philippe Ariès's *Centuries of Childhood*
Franz Boas's *Race, Language and Culture*
Kim Chan & Renée Mauborgne's *Blue Ocean Strategy*
Jared Diamond's *Guns, Germs & Steel: the Fate of Human Societies*
Jared Diamond's *Collapse: How Societies Choose to Fail or Survive*
E. E. Evans-Pritchard's *Witchcraft, Oracles and Magic Among the Azande*
James Ferguson's *The Anti-Politics Machine*
Clifford Geertz's *The Interpretation of Cultures*
David Graeber's *Debt: the First 5000 Years*
Karen Ho's *Liquidated: An Ethnography of Wall Street*
Geert Hofstede's *Culture's Consequences: Comparing Values, Behaviors, Institutes and Organizations across Nations*
Claude Lévi-Strauss's *Structural Anthropology*
Jay Macleod's *Ain't No Makin' It: Aspirations and Attainment in a Low-Income Neighborhood*
Saba Mahmood's *The Politics of Piety: The Islamic Revival and the Feminist Subject*
Marcel Mauss's *The Gift*

BUSINESS

Jean Lave & Etienne Wenger's *Situated Learning*
Theodore Levitt's *Marketing Myopia*
Burton G. Malkiel's *A Random Walk Down Wall Street*
Douglas McGregor's *The Human Side of Enterprise*
Michael Porter's *Competitive Strategy: Creating and Sustaining Superior Performance*
John Kotter's *Leading Change*
C. K. Prahalad & Gary Hamel's *The Core Competence of the Corporation*

CRIMINOLOGY

Michelle Alexander's *The New Jim Crow: Mass Incarceration in the Age of Colorblindness*
Michael R. Gottfredson & Travis Hirschi's *A General Theory of Crime*
Richard Herrnstein & Charles A. Murray's *The Bell Curve: Intelligence and Class Structure in American Life*
Elizabeth Loftus's *Eyewitness Testimony*
Jay Macleod's *Ain't No Makin' It: Aspirations and Attainment in a Low-Income Neighborhood*
Philip Zimbardo's *The Lucifer Effect*

ECONOMICS

Janet Abu-Lughod's *Before European Hegemony*
Ha-Joon Chang's *Kicking Away the Ladder*
David Brion Davis's *The Problem of Slavery in the Age of Revolution*
Milton Friedman's *The Role of Monetary Policy*
Milton Friedman's *Capitalism and Freedom*
David Graeber's *Debt: the First 5000 Years*
Friedrich Hayek's *The Road to Serfdom*
Karen Ho's *Liquidated: An Ethnography of Wall Street*

The Macat Library By Discipline

John Maynard Keynes's *The General Theory of Employment, Interest and Money*
Charles P. Kindleberger's *Manias, Panics and Crashes*
Robert Lucas's *Why Doesn't Capital Flow from Rich to Poor Countries?*
Burton G. Malkiel's *A Random Walk Down Wall Street*
Thomas Robert Malthus's *An Essay on the Principle of Population*
Karl Marx's *Capital*
Thomas Piketty's *Capital in the Twenty-First Century*
Amartya Sen's *Development as Freedom*
Adam Smith's *The Wealth of Nations*
Nassim Nicholas Taleb's *The Black Swan: The Impact of the Highly Improbable*
Amos Tversky's & Daniel Kahneman's *Judgment under Uncertainty: Heuristics and Biases*
Mahbub Ul Haq's *Reflections on Human Development*
Max Weber's *The Protestant Ethic and the Spirit of Capitalism*

FEMINISM AND GENDER STUDIES

Judith Butler's *Gender Trouble*
Simone De Beauvoir's *The Second Sex*
Michel Foucault's *History of Sexuality*
Betty Friedan's *The Feminine Mystique*
Saba Mahmood's *The Politics of Piety: The Islamic Revival and the Feminist Subject*
Joan Wallach Scott's *Gender and the Politics of History*
Mary Wollstonecraft's *A Vindication of the Rights of Woman*
Virginia Woolf's *A Room of One's Own*

GEOGRAPHY

The Brundtland Report's *Our Common Future*
Rachel Carson's *Silent Spring*
Charles Darwin's *On the Origin of Species*
James Ferguson's *The Anti-Politics Machine*
Jane Jacobs's *The Death and Life of Great American Cities*
James Lovelock's *Gaia: A New Look at Life on Earth*
Amartya Sen's *Development as Freedom*
Mathis Wackernagel & William Rees's *Our Ecological Footprint*

HISTORY

Janet Abu-Lughod's *Before European Hegemony*
Benedict Anderson's *Imagined Communities*
Bernard Bailyn's *The Ideological Origins of the American Revolution*
Hanna Batatu's *The Old Social Classes And The Revolutionary Movements Of Iraq*
Christopher Browning's *Ordinary Men: Reserve Police Batallion 101 and the Final Solution in Poland*
Edmund Burke's *Reflections on the Revolution in France*
William Cronon's *Nature's Metropolis: Chicago And The Great West*
Alfred W. Crosby's *The Columbian Exchange*
Hamid Dabashi's *Iran: A People Interrupted*
David Brion Davis's *The Problem of Slavery in the Age of Revolution*
Nathalie Zemon Davis's *The Return of Martin Guerre*
Jared Diamond's *Guns, Germs & Steel: the Fate of Human Societies*
Frank Dikotter's *Mao's Great Famine*
John W Dower's *War Without Mercy: Race And Power In The Pacific War*
W. E. B. Du Bois's *The Souls of Black Folk*
Richard J. Evans's *In Defence of History*
Lucien Febvre's *The Problem of Unbelief in the 16th Century*
Sheila Fitzpatrick's *Everyday Stalinism*

Eric Foner's *Reconstruction: America's Unfinished Revolution, 1863-1877*
Michel Foucault's *Discipline and Punish*
Michel Foucault's *History of Sexuality*
Francis Fukuyama's *The End of History and the Last Man*
John Lewis Gaddis's *We Now Know: Rethinking Cold War History*
Ernest Gellner's *Nations and Nationalism*
Eugene Genovese's *Roll, Jordan, Roll: The World the Slaves Made*
Carlo Ginzburg's *The Night Battles*
Daniel Goldhagen's *Hitler's Willing Executioners*
Jack Goldstone's *Revolution and Rebellion in the Early Modern World*
Antonio Gramsci's *The Prison Notebooks*
Alexander Hamilton, John Jay & James Madison's *The Federalist Papers*
Christopher Hill's *The World Turned Upside Down*
Carole Hillenbrand's *The Crusades: Islamic Perspectives*
Thomas Hobbes's *Leviathan*
Eric Hobsbawm's *The Age Of Revolution*
John A. Hobson's *Imperialism: A Study*
Albert Hourani's *History of the Arab Peoples*
Samuel P. Huntington's *The Clash of Civilizations and the Remaking of World Order*
C. L. R. James's *The Black Jacobins*
Tony Judt's *Postwar: A History of Europe Since 1945*
Ernst Kantorowicz's *The King's Two Bodies: A Study in Medieval Political Theology*
Paul Kennedy's *The Rise and Fall of the Great Powers*
Ian Kershaw's *The "Hitler Myth": Image and Reality in the Third Reich*
John Maynard Keynes's *The General Theory of Employment, Interest and Money*
Charles P. Kindleberger's *Manias, Panics and Crashes*
Martin Luther King Jr's *Why We Can't Wait*
Henry Kissinger's *World Order: Reflections on the Character of Nations and the Course of History*
Thomas Kuhn's *The Structure of Scientific Revolutions*
Georges Lefebvre's *The Coming of the French Revolution*
John Locke's *Two Treatises of Government*
Niccolò Machiavelli's *The Prince*
Thomas Robert Malthus's *An Essay on the Principle of Population*
Mahmood Mamdani's *Citizen and Subject: Contemporary Africa And The Legacy Of Late Colonialism*
Karl Marx's *Capital*
Stanley Milgram's *Obedience to Authority*
John Stuart Mill's *On Liberty*
Thomas Paine's *Common Sense*
Thomas Paine's *Rights of Man*
Geoffrey Parker's *Global Crisis: War, Climate Change and Catastrophe in the Seventeenth Century*
Jonathan Riley-Smith's *The First Crusade and the Idea of Crusading*
Jean-Jacques Rousseau's *The Social Contract*
Joan Wallach Scott's *Gender and the Politics of History*
Theda Skocpol's *States and Social Revolutions*
Adam Smith's *The Wealth of Nations*
Timothy Snyder's *Bloodlands: Europe Between Hitler and Stalin*
Sun Tzu's *The Art of War*
Keith Thomas's *Religion and the Decline of Magic*
Thucydides's *The History of the Peloponnesian War*
Frederick Jackson Turner's *The Significance of the Frontier in American History*
Odd Arne Westad's *The Global Cold War: Third World Interventions And The Making Of Our Times*

The Macat Library By Discipline

LITERATURE

Chinua Achebe's *An Image of Africa: Racism in Conrad's Heart of Darkness*
Roland Barthes's *Mythologies*
Homi K. Bhabha's *The Location of Culture*
Judith Butler's *Gender Trouble*
Simone De Beauvoir's *The Second Sex*
Ferdinand De Saussure's *Course in General Linguistics*
T. S. Eliot's *The Sacred Wood: Essays on Poetry and Criticism*
Zora Neale Huston's *Characteristics of Negro Expression*
Toni Morrison's *Playing in the Dark: Whiteness in the American Literary Imagination*
Edward Said's *Orientalism*
Gayatri Chakravorty Spivak's *Can the Subaltern Speak?*
Mary Wollstonecraft's *A Vindication of the Rights of Women*
Virginia Woolf's *A Room of One's Own*

PHILOSOPHY

Elizabeth Anscombe's *Modern Moral Philosophy*
Hannah Arendt's *The Human Condition*
Aristotle's *Metaphysics*
Aristotle's *Nicomachean Ethics*
Edmund Gettier's *Is Justified True Belief Knowledge?*
Georg Wilhelm Friedrich Hegel's *Phenomenology of Spirit*
David Hume's *Dialogues Concerning Natural Religion*
David Hume's *The Enquiry for Human Understanding*
Immanuel Kant's *Religion within the Boundaries of Mere Reason*
Immanuel Kant's *Critique of Pure Reason*
Søren Kierkegaard's *The Sickness Unto Death*
Søren Kierkegaard's *Fear and Trembling*
C. S. Lewis's *The Abolition of Man*
Alasdair MacIntyre's *After Virtue*
Marcus Aurelius's *Meditations*
Friedrich Nietzsche's *On the Genealogy of Morality*
Friedrich Nietzsche's *Beyond Good and Evil*
Plato's *Republic*
Plato's *Symposium*
Jean-Jacques Rousseau's *The Social Contract*
Gilbert Ryle's *The Concept of Mind*
Baruch Spinoza's *Ethics*
Sun Tzu's *The Art of War*
Ludwig Wittgenstein's *Philosophical Investigations*

POLITICS

Benedict Anderson's *Imagined Communities*
Aristotle's *Politics*
Bernard Bailyn's *The Ideological Origins of the American Revolution*
Edmund Burke's *Reflections on the Revolution in France*
John C. Calhoun's *A Disquisition on Government*
Ha-Joon Chang's *Kicking Away the Ladder*
Hamid Dabashi's *Iran: A People Interrupted*
Hamid Dabashi's *Theology of Discontent: The Ideological Foundation of the Islamic Revolution in Iran*
Robert Dahl's *Democracy and its Critics*
Robert Dahl's *Who Governs?*
David Brion Davis's *The Problem of Slavery in the Age of Revolution*

Alexis De Tocqueville's *Democracy in America*
James Ferguson's *The Anti-Politics Machine*
Frank Dikotter's *Mao's Great Famine*
Sheila Fitzpatrick's *Everyday Stalinism*
Eric Foner's *Reconstruction: America's Unfinished Revolution, 1863-1877*
Milton Friedman's *Capitalism and Freedom*
Francis Fukuyama's *The End of History and the Last Man*
John Lewis Gaddis's *We Now Know: Rethinking Cold War History*
Ernest Gellner's *Nations and Nationalism*
David Graeber's *Debt: the First 5000 Years*
Antonio Gramsci's *The Prison Notebooks*
Alexander Hamilton, John Jay & James Madison's *The Federalist Papers*
Friedrich Hayek's *The Road to Serfdom*
Christopher Hill's *The World Turned Upside Down*
Thomas Hobbes's *Leviathan*
John A. Hobson's *Imperialism: A Study*
Samuel P. Huntington's *The Clash of Civilizations and the Remaking of World Order*
Tony Judt's *Postwar: A History of Europe Since 1945*
David C. Kang's *China Rising: Peace, Power and Order in East Asia*
Paul Kennedy's *The Rise and Fall of Great Powers*
Robert Keohane's *After Hegemony*
Martin Luther King Jr.'s *Why We Can't Wait*
Henry Kissinger's *World Order: Reflections on the Character of Nations and the Course of History*
John Locke's *Two Treatises of Government*
Niccolò Machiavelli's *The Prince*
Thomas Robert Malthus's *An Essay on the Principle of Population*
Mahmood Mamdani's *Citizen and Subject: Contemporary Africa And The Legacy Of Late Colonialism*
Karl Marx's *Capital*
John Stuart Mill's *On Liberty*
John Stuart Mill's *Utilitarianism*
Hans Morgenthau's *Politics Among Nations*
Thomas Paine's *Common Sense*
Thomas Paine's *Rights of Man*
Thomas Piketty's *Capital in the Twenty-First Century*
Robert D. Putman's *Bowling Alone*
John Rawls's *Theory of Justice*
Jean-Jacques Rousseau's *The Social Contract*
Theda Skocpol's *States and Social Revolutions*
Adam Smith's *The Wealth of Nations*
Sun Tzu's *The Art of War*
Henry David Thoreau's *Civil Disobedience*
Thucydides's *The History of the Peloponnesian War*
Kenneth Waltz's *Theory of International Politics*
Max Weber's *Politics as a Vocation*
Odd Arne Westad's *The Global Cold War: Third World Interventions And The Making Of Our Times*

POSTCOLONIAL STUDIES

Roland Barthes's *Mythologies*
Frantz Fanon's *Black Skin, White Masks*
Homi K. Bhabha's *The Location of Culture*
Gustavo Gutiérrez's *A Theology of Liberation*
Edward Said's *Orientalism*
Gayatri Chakravorty Spivak's *Can the Subaltern Speak?*

The Macat Library By Discipline

PSYCHOLOGY

Gordon Allport's *The Nature of Prejudice*
Alan Baddeley & Graham Hitch's *Aggression: A Social Learning Analysis*
Albert Bandura's *Aggression: A Social Learning Analysis*
Leon Festinger's *A Theory of Cognitive Dissonance*
Sigmund Freud's *The Interpretation of Dreams*
Betty Friedan's *The Feminine Mystique*
Michael R. Gottfredson & Travis Hirschi's *A General Theory of Crime*
Eric Hoffer's *The True Believer: Thoughts on the Nature of Mass Movements*
William James's *Principles of Psychology*
Elizabeth Loftus's *Eyewitness Testimony*
A. H. Maslow's *A Theory of Human Motivation*
Stanley Milgram's *Obedience to Authority*
Steven Pinker's *The Better Angels of Our Nature*
Oliver Sacks's *The Man Who Mistook His Wife For a Hat*
Richard Thaler & Cass Sunstein's *Nudge: Improving Decisions About Health, Wealth and Happiness*
Amos Tversky's *Judgment under Uncertainty: Heuristics and Biases*
Philip Zimbardo's *The Lucifer Effect*

SCIENCE

Rachel Carson's *Silent Spring*
William Cronon's *Nature's Metropolis: Chicago And The Great West*
Alfred W. Crosby's *The Columbian Exchange*
Charles Darwin's *On the Origin of Species*
Richard Dawkin's *The Selfish Gene*
Thomas Kuhn's *The Structure of Scientific Revolutions*
Geoffrey Parker's *Global Crisis: War, Climate Change and Catastrophe in the Seventeenth Century*
Mathis Wackernagel & William Rees's *Our Ecological Footprint*

SOCIOLOGY

Michelle Alexander's *The New Jim Crow: Mass Incarceration in the Age of Colorblindness*
Gordon Allport's *The Nature of Prejudice*
Albert Bandura's *Aggression: A Social Learning Analysis*
Hanna Batatu's *The Old Social Classes And The Revolutionary Movements Of Iraq*
Ha-Joon Chang's *Kicking Away the Ladder*
W. E. B. Du Bois's *The Souls of Black Folk*
Émile Durkheim's *On Suicide*
Frantz Fanon's *Black Skin, White Masks*
Frantz Fanon's *The Wretched of the Earth*
Eric Foner's *Reconstruction: America's Unfinished Revolution, 1863-1877*
Eugene Genovese's *Roll, Jordan, Roll: The World the Slaves Made*
Jack Goldstone's *Revolution and Rebellion in the Early Modern World*
Antonio Gramsci's *The Prison Notebooks*
Richard Herrnstein & Charles A Murray's *The Bell Curve: Intelligence and Class Structure in American Life*
Eric Hoffer's *The True Believer: Thoughts on the Nature of Mass Movements*
Jane Jacobs's *The Death and Life of Great American Cities*
Robert Lucas's *Why Doesn't Capital Flow from Rich to Poor Countries?*
Jay Macleod's *Ain't No Makin' It: Aspirations and Attainment in a Low Income Neighborhood*
Elaine May's *Homeward Bound: American Families in the Cold War Era*
Douglas McGregor's *The Human Side of Enterprise*
C. Wright Mills's *The Sociological Imagination*

Thomas Piketty's *Capital in the Twenty-First Century*
Robert D. Putman's *Bowling Alone*
David Riesman's *The Lonely Crowd: A Study of the Changing American Character*
Edward Said's *Orientalism*
Joan Wallach Scott's *Gender and the Politics of History*
Theda Skocpol's *States and Social Revolutions*
Max Weber's *The Protestant Ethic and the Spirit of Capitalism*

THEOLOGY

Augustine's *Confessions*
Benedict's *Rule of St Benedict*
Gustavo Gutiérrez's *A Theology of Liberation*
Carole Hillenbrand's *The Crusades: Islamic Perspectives*
David Hume's *Dialogues Concerning Natural Religion*
Immanuel Kant's *Religion within the Boundaries of Mere Reason*
Ernst Kantorowicz's *The King's Two Bodies: A Study in Medieval Political Theology*
Søren Kierkegaard's *The Sickness Unto Death*
C. S. Lewis's *The Abolition of Man*
Saba Mahmood's *The Politics of Piety: The Islamic Revival and the Feminist Subject*
Baruch Spinoza's *Ethics*
Keith Thomas's *Religion and the Decline of Magic*

COMING SOON

Chris Argyris's *The Individual and the Organisation*
Seyla Benhabib's *The Rights of Others*
Walter Benjamin's *The Work Of Art in the Age of Mechanical Reproduction*
John Berger's *Ways of Seeing*
Pierre Bourdieu's *Outline of a Theory of Practice*
Mary Douglas's *Purity and Danger*
Roland Dworkin's *Taking Rights Seriously*
James G. March's *Exploration and Exploitation in Organisational Learning*
Ikujiro Nonaka's *A Dynamic Theory of Organizational Knowledge Creation*
Griselda Pollock's *Vision and Difference*
Amartya Sen's *Inequality Re-Examined*
Susan Sontag's *On Photography*
Yasser Tabbaa's *The Transformation of Islamic Art*
Ludwig von Mises's *Theory of Money and Credit*

Macat Disciplines

Access the greatest ideas and thinkers across entire disciplines, including

FEMINISM, GENDER AND QUEER STUDIES

Simone De Beauvoir's
The Second Sex

Michel Foucault's
History of Sexuality

Betty Friedan's
The Feminine Mystique

Saba Mahmood's
*The Politics of Piety:
The Islamic Revival and
the Feminist Subject*

Joan Wallach Scott's
*Gender and the
Politics of History*

Mary Wollstonecraft's
*A Vindication of the
Rights of Woman*

Virginia Woolf's
A Room of One's Own

Judith Butler's
Gender Trouble

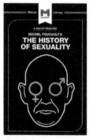

Macat analyses are available from all good bookshops and libraries.

Access hundreds of analyses through one, multimedia tool.
Join free for one month **library.macat.com**

Macat Disciplines

Access the greatest ideas and thinkers across entire disciplines, including

CRIMINOLOGY

Michelle Alexander's
*The New Jim Crow:
Mass Incarceration in the
Age of Colorblindness*

**Michael R. Gottfredson
& Travis Hirschi's**
A General Theory of Crime

Elizabeth Loftus's
Eyewitness Testimony

**Richard Herrnstein
& Charles A. Murray's**
*The Bell Curve: Intelligence and
Class Structure in American Life*

Jay Macleod's
*Ain't No Makin' It:
Aspirations and Attainment in a
Low-Income Neighborhood*

Philip Zimbardo's
The Lucifer Effect

Macat Disciplines

Access the greatest ideas and thinkers across entire disciplines, including

Postcolonial Studies

Roland Barthes's *Mythologies*
Frantz Fanon's *Black Skin, White Masks*
Homi K. Bhabha's *The Location of Culture*
Gustavo Gutiérrez's *A Theology of Liberation*
Edward Said's *Orientalism*
Gayatri Chakravorty Spivak's *Can the Subaltern Speak?*

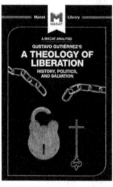

Macat analyses are available from all good bookshops and libraries.

Access hundreds of analyses through one, multimedia tool.
Join free for one month **library.macat.com**

Macat Disciplines

Access the greatest ideas and thinkers across entire disciplines, including

GLOBALIZATION

Arjun Appadurai's, *Modernity at Large: Cultural Dimensions of Globalisation*

James Ferguson's, *The Anti-Politics Machine*

Geert Hofstede's, *Culture's Consequences*

Amartya Sen's, *Development as Freedom*

Macat analyses are available from all good bookshops and libraries.

Access hundreds of analyses through one, multimedia tool.
Join free for one month **library.macat.com**

Macat Pairs

Analyse historical and modern issues from opposite sides of an argument. Pairs include:

HOW TO RUN AN ECONOMY

John Maynard Keynes's
The General Theory OF Employment, Interest and Money

Classical economics suggests that market economies are self-correcting in times of recession or depression, and tend toward full employment and output. But English economist John Maynard Keynes disagrees.

In his ground-breaking 1936 study *The General Theory*, Keynes argues that traditional economics has misunderstood the causes of unemployment. Employment is not determined by the price of labor; it is directly linked to demand. Keynes believes market economies are by nature unstable, and so require government intervention. Spurred on by the social catastrophe of the Great Depression of the 1930s, he sets out to revolutionize the way the world thinks

Milton Friedman's
The Role of Monetary Policy

Friedman's 1968 paper changed the course of economic theory. In just 17 pages, he demolished existing theory and outlined an effective alternate monetary policy designed to secure 'high employment, stable prices and rapid growth.'

Friedman demonstrated that monetary policy plays a vital role in broader economic stability and argued that economists got their monetary policy wrong in the 1950s and 1960s by misunderstanding the relationship between inflation and unemployment. Previous generations of economists had believed that governments could permanently decrease unemployment by permitting inflation—and vice versa. Friedman's most original contribution was to show that this supposed trade-off is an illusion that only works in the short term.

Macat analyses are available from all good bookshops and libraries.

Access hundreds of analyses through one, multimedia tool.
Join free for one month **library.macat.com**

Macat Disciplines

Access the greatest ideas and thinkers across entire disciplines, including

AFRICANA STUDIES

Chinua Achebe's *An Image of Africa: Racism in Conrad's Heart of Darkness*

W. E. B. Du Bois's *The Souls of Black Folk*

Zora Neale Hurston's *Characteristics of Negro Expression*

Martin Luther King Jr.'s *Why We Can't Wait*

Toni Morrison's *Playing in the Dark: Whiteness in the American Literary Imagination*

Macat analyses are available from all good bookshops and libraries.

Access hundreds of analyses through one, multimedia tool.
Join free for one month **library.macat.com**

Macat Disciplines

Access the greatest ideas and thinkers across entire disciplines, including

THE FUTURE OF DEMOCRACY

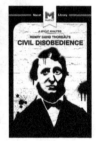

Robert A. Dahl's, *Democracy and Its Critics*
Robert A. Dahl's, *Who Governs?*
Alexis De Toqueville's, *Democracy in America*
Niccolò Machiavelli's, *The Prince*
John Stuart Mill's, *On Liberty*
Robert D. Putnam's, *Bowling Alone*
Jean-Jacques Rousseau's, *The Social Contract*
Henry David Thoreau's, *Civil Disobedience*

Macat Disciplines

Access the greatest ideas and thinkers across entire disciplines, including

TOTALITARIANISM

Sheila Fitzpatrick's, *Everyday Stalinism*
Ian Kershaw's, *The "Hitler Myth"*
Timothy Snyder's, *Bloodlands*

Macat Disciplines

Access the greatest ideas and thinkers across entire disciplines, including

INEQUALITY

Ha-Joon Chang's, *Kicking Away the Ladder*
David Graeber's, *Debt: The First 5000 Years*
Robert E. Lucas's, *Why Doesn't Capital Flow from Rich To Poor Countries?*
Thomas Piketty's, *Capital in the Twenty-First Century*
Amartya Sen's, *Inequality Re-Examined*
Mahbub Ul Haq's, *Reflections on Human Development*

Macat analyses are available from all good bookshops and libraries.

Access hundreds of analyses through one, multimedia tool.
Join free for one month **library.macat.com**

Macat Pairs

Analyse historical and modern issues from opposite sides of an argument. Pairs include:

RACE AND IDENTITY

Zora Neale Hurston's
Characteristics of Negro Expression

Using material collected on anthropological expeditions to the South, Zora Neale Hurston explains how expression in African American culture in the early twentieth century departs from the art of white America. At the time, African American art was often criticized for copying white culture. For Hurston, this criticism misunderstood how art works. European tradition views art as something fixed. But Hurston describes a creative process that is alive, ever-changing, and largely improvisational. She maintains that African American art works through a process called 'mimicry'—where an imitated object or verbal pattern, for example, is reshaped and altered until it becomes something new, novel—and worthy of attention.

Frantz Fanon's
Black Skin, White Masks

Black Skin, White Masks offers a radical analysis of the psychological effects of colonization on the colonized.

Fanon witnessed the effects of colonization first hand both in his birthplace, Martinique, and again later in life when he worked as a psychiatrist in another French colony, Algeria. His text is uncompromising in form and argument. He dissects the dehumanizing effects of colonialism, arguing that it destroys the native sense of identity, forcing people to adapt to an alien set of values—including a core belief that they are inferior. This results in deep psychological trauma.

Fanon's work played a pivotal role in the civil rights movements of the 1960s.

Macat Disciplines

Access the greatest ideas and thinkers across entire disciplines, including

MAN AND THE ENVIRONMENT

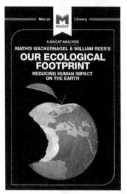

The Brundtland Report's, *Our Common Future*
Rachel Carson's, *Silent Spring*
James Lovelock's, *Gaia: A New Look at Life on Earth*
Mathis Wackernagel & William Rees's, *Our Ecological Footprint*

Macat analyses are available from all good bookshops and libraries.

Access hundreds of analyses through one, multimedia tool.
Join free for one month **library.macat.com**

Macat Pairs

Analyse historical and modern issues from opposite sides of an argument. Pairs include:

INTERNATIONAL RELATIONS IN THE 21ST CENTURY

Samuel P. Huntington's
The Clash of Civilisations

In his highly influential 1996 book, Huntington offers a vision of a post-Cold War world in which conflict takes place not between competing ideologies but between cultures. The worst clash, he argues, will be between the Islamic world and the West: the West's arrogance and belief that its culture is a "gift" to the world will come into conflict with Islam's obstinacy and concern that its culture is under attack from a morally decadent "other."

Clash inspired much debate between different political schools of thought. But its greatest impact came in helping define American foreign policy in the wake of the 2001 terrorist attacks in New York and Washington.

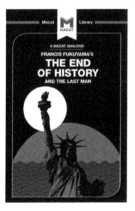

Francis Fukuyama's
The End of History and the Last Man

Published in 1992, *The End of History and the Last Man* argues that capitalist democracy is the final destination for all societies. Fukuyama believed democracy triumphed during the Cold War because it lacks the "fundamental contradictions" inherent in communism and satisfies our yearning for freedom and equality. Democracy therefore marks the endpoint in the evolution of ideology, and so the "end of history." There will still be "events," but no fundamental change in ideology.

Printed in the United States
by Baker & Taylor Publisher Services